THE OTHER SIDE
OF THE MOUNTAIN

Charleston, SC
www.PalmettoPublishing.com

Charleston, SC
www.PalmettoPublishing.com

The Other Side of the Mountain
Copyright © 2023 by Marion Devoe Sr.

First Edition

Hardcover ISBN: 979-8-8229-1416-2
Paperback ISBN: 979-8-8229-1417-9

THE
OTHER SIDE
OF THE
MOUNTAIN

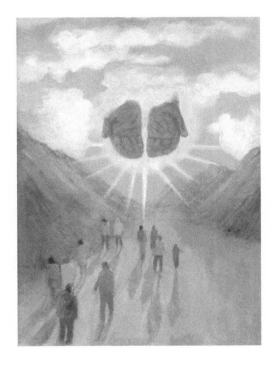

THIS BOOK WILL
CHANGE YOUR LIFE
MARION DEVOE SR.

PRAISE FOR

THE OTHER SIDE OF THE MOUNTAIN

Marion Devoe writes from a source rooted in his faith, his commitment to family, and a lifetime of experiences, which include overcoming seemingly insurmountable odds. He has seen good things in life and has also come up close and personal with man's inhumanity to man—from hearing of its presence in the garden of Eden, then on to Calvary; to living it on the battlefield and knowing that it is ever-present today—even in our most sacred places. In this book Marion Devoe boldly tackles some of the "hard stuff," including practices that seem to have turned a deaf ear to the basic tenet of "doing unto others as you would have done unto you." His point of view is thought-provoking and may push buttons, but read with an open mind, inspires us to think beyond ourselves and to earnestly embrace practical and positive means of uplifting and supporting others through challenging life experiences.

—Jannie Busby, MEd, retired administrative coordinator, Savannah-Chatham County Public Schools, Department of Special Education

◇◇

Marion is a remarkable man whose skill as a writer has produced both riveting and captivating storylines. This work contributes to the African American journey as we continue to examine who we are as a people. His ability to capture the essence of our human condition is phenomenal.

—Beverly Davis, MBA, author of *The Road to Redemption*

◇◇

> "Yea, though I walk through the valley of the shadow of death, I will fear no evil: for thou art with me; thy rod and thy staff they comfort me." —Psalm 23:4

This book is an actual demonstration of how combined faith and belief in God and self, will overcome our mountains and valleys in life.

—Julius Larry III, DDS, JD

◇◇

The Other Side of the Mountain vividly illustrates how God helps us as we are confronted with mountains and valleys. No one is exempt from valleys and situations, but relying on God's directions can make the impossible, possible.

—Bonnie L. Young, MEd, retired educator

◇◇

Marion and I were high school classmates. Reading his life story in his first book, *Never Give Up*, was inspiring. We are fortunate that he is using his faith and experiences to teach others how to navigate life's obstacles. For young people in the prime of life, this book can help guide them to success. For the more mature, this book can remind us that we have the strength to overcome our obstacles. It also reminds us that God is on our side. Thank you, Marion.

—Jacqueline Hall Hopkins, EdD, retired educator/school board member, Hampton County School District, Estill, South Carolina

As a loving husband and supportive father with his strong Christian faith, Marion has taken on the task of writing and giving meaning to the mountains and valleys we all journey through in life. I have shared his writings with members of my family, and I highly recommend this book to those seeking ways to navigate life's journey through the mountains and valleys.

—Deacon Anthony J. Weaver, civil marriage celebrant

As Marion Devoe's former teacher at Tompkins High School in Savannah, Georgia, I am truly amazed at his resilience and persistence and the inspirational stories he illustrates in this book. I encourage others to use this book as a roadmap for their life's journey to the other side of the mountain.

—Mr. Alex Habersham, MEd, educator

My journey in life took me up many mountains and through many valleys. But by faith I continued on and reached every goal. Faith and action are the basis of life. Faith is when you do your part and leave the rest to God. This book by my friend Marion Devoe paints a beautiful picture of how your faith can move mountains as you journey to the other side of the mountain in life.

—**Andrew Forte, MBA, retired CPA**

DEDICATION
In the Memory of

Michael Devoe

and

Alexis Devoe.

THIS BOOK IS ALSO DEDICATED TO MY NINE SIBLINGS:

Gladys Devoe Holmes

Glenda Devoe Williams

Frank Devoe

Ann Devoe

Mayda Devoe

Lamar Devoe

Lamore Devoe

Algier Devoe

Gerald Devoe

TABLE OF CONTENTS

FOREWORD

◇◇◇◇◇◇◇◇◇◇◇◇◇◇◇◇◇◇◇◇◇◇◇◇◇

AS A CHILD I enjoyed reading novels by British novelist Roald Dahl. Most people would be familiar with his famous novel, *Charlie and the Chocolate Factory*. However, the novel of his that I adored the most was titled *The BFG* (short for the Big Friendly Giant). The BFG just so happens to be my six-foot-eight tall father. A man of great stature, kindness, and wisdom, and the author of the book you are about to embark on.

The message in this book is not the typical motivational message you may find in your average inspirational literature. Reaching goals and aspirations in life is not as simple as having so-called "grit." Unless you were born in another galaxy somewhere, we are all human. As part of the human living condition, we will all encounter high and low experiences, and in the case of this book, mountains and valleys. As I think about my life and some of the challenges that I have faced, I wouldn't be where I am today without the wisdom and knowledge that my father instilled in me. This book is a real gift to anyone who may deal with fears or other scenarios or ordeals that seem impossible to surmount. The chapters ahead will help you recognize the different types of mountains you will face in your life journey and assist you with navigating them, while avoiding missteps along the way. It will also serve as a beacon of light for the dark times in the valley, where giving up may seem like the only real option.

Perhaps it was a conversation with my father after I didn't make the basketball team or a phone call with him explaining I didn't land my dream job. He always knew the right words to say to encourage me to want more and continue on my journey. I've faced all elements of this book and attribute my positive career development to the teachings of my father. This book will make you wiser but also help you embrace and appreciate your personal journey through the mountains and valleys of life.

—Jon Devoe, vice president of growth and development, Yieldlove

FOREWORD

I AM HONORED to have been asked by my friend Marion Devoe to write a foreword for his second book, *The Other Side of the Mountain*. I have known Marion and his wife, Ann, since 2016. Together we serve our church in Vienna, Virginia, as Stephen Ministers: a lay ministry of members who are trained and certified to provide one-to-one Christian care to people who are experiencing a difficult time in life.

This book addresses the challenging mountains and valleys that we all experience during our lifetime. The reader will be engaged and encouraged as Marion shares honestly and sincerely about events that have shaped him during his own journey. Through storytelling interwoven with scripture, encouraging words, humor, and life lessons learned, he reveals his heart for giving wise counsel to people who are going through the mountains and valleys of life. Look for the gems found throughout the book!

Here are some that I found:

- In our valley of hard times, it is only when we fix our eyes on God that we will find the way out of the valley and the peace that we desire.

- Even when we can't see the goodness of God's plan, it's still there. He has already gone before you and made your path straight for His blessing for you. So keep going and follow His path, and every step you take will lead you closer to His will and the blessing He has for you.
- Most of all: Be encouraged, and never give up!

—Sylvia Taylor, retired teacher, historian, and Stephen Minister

PREFACE

◇◇◇◇◇◇◇◇◇◇◇◇◇◇◇◇◇◇

WE WILL HAVE obstacles and mountains before us as we journey through life. "The mountains in our lives are not the earthly mountains, but the mountains of man." Our mountains and valleys are life's realities, and we must learn to live with them. In this analogy, consider that we want to be on the mountaintops all the time and avoid the deep valleys in our lives. We may fail to realize that to reach the mountaintop we must first climb upward on many rough and winding trails. Once we do reach the mountaintops, if we desire to continue on with life, then we must move forward, which will require that we head back down into the valleys. Each valley in our lives has a purpose.

Most of us do tend to associate difficult times in our lives with the idea of being in a valley. Maybe it's a time of depression or despair. Maybe you've lost your job or are struggling financially. Maybe your job performance is just suffering. Maybe it's a relationship that is broken and appears to be shattered. Whatever valley you are in today, God is your Shepherd. He will take you up the mountains and guide you through the valleys in your life.

This is the second edition of my first book, *Never Give Up*. I hope this book will help you overcome the mountains and valleys in your life. Throughout my life's journey through America and other parts of the world, I have seen and experienced many mountains and valleys, which leads me to believe that people are the same wherever I travel. They are of one blood and want the same things in life as I do, whether they are in Cape Town, South Africa; Sydney, Australia; Hamburg, Germany; South Vietnam; Trinidad; or a small town in Wisconsin. The one difference is that they may speak a different language or dialect relative to their particular region of the world, but their meanings are the same. The things we all have in common are the mountains and valleys in our lives and the challenges that come with them. The mountains in our lives are not God's earthly mountains but are metaphors for things that obstruct us in our lives. The valleys are metaphors for the highs and lows, struggles, and darkest times in our life's journey.

> *Trust in the Lord with all your heart, and do not rely on your understanding. Acknowledge him in all your ways, and he will make your paths straight.* (Proverbs 3:5)

INTRODUCTION

◇◇◇◇◇◇◇◇◇◇◇◇◇◇◇◇◇◇◇◇◇◇◇◇◇◇◇◇◇◇◇◇◇◇

AS WE JOURNEY through this life, our mountains and valleys will appear before us, casting shadows; creating doubt, fears, and storms; and flooding the valleys of our minds with pain and hardships.

The mountains in our lives are from man's evil and conscious intent and will serve only to lure you into the realms of hell without ever leading you to your purpose, and to your direction in life.

God's creations of earthly mountains are majestically beautiful and are situated like murals on earth's vast landscape.

Man-created mountains are the ones you see in your everyday life and are from the evil and conscious intent of man.

In this life, be conscious of people you may know and trust because they may be your earthly mountains, your enemies, haters, and the barriers to your life's success and happiness.

1

THE MOUNTAINS IN OUR LIVES

◇◇◇◇◇◇◇◇◇◇◇◇◇◇◇◇◇◇◇◇◇◇◇◇◇◇◇◇◇

WE ALL WILL experience mountains and valleys at some point in our lives. The mountains are from the actual people, places, and things that surround us; they symbolize our ups and downs, and we struggle to overcome them.

Our mountains also arise from our aspirations, our goals, and desires. I hope that this book will enable you to climb every mountain and walk through every valley of your life and be blessed. Let's start your journey up the mountains and through the valleys. The mountains before man are from his aspirations and goals and are constructed as a result of selfish desires, attitudes, anger, bitterness, and hate.

Some mountains in our lives are from the consequences of retribution theology. Remarks John Tulloch, "Retribution theology is the belief that those who are obedient to God are called righteous and will be blessed, while those that are disobedient are wicked and will be cursed" (2006).

The beautiful earthly mountains are capped with white snow, while the mountains of man have been around for a long time and are now no longer capped under a white cloak. Some man-made mountains are from the people in your life, even those close to you.

We all will experience ups and downs in our lives, but we don't go through them alone. God has promised to be with us every step of the way. The earthly mountains today are from our hate, power, greed, and political and judicial systems, spewing dark clouds of despair across America and eroding the democratic norms. These mountains before us are creating a climate of corrosiveness and inequality across America and are therefore darkening the beacon, the light, of one of the greatest nations on earth.

With the help of our God, we all will deal with these mountains before us. Yet each day in our lifetime, we will wake up each morning and start to go about our day, and, before we place our feet on the floor, an unknown mountain and a cloud of despair will appear before us and darken our days like the mountain before you now. Today in America we are faced with so many uncertainties, with mountains of problems, hate, and stress in our daily lives. I am here to tell you that we all can rise to the peak of each mountain with God's grace and mercy. When God does not move the mountain before you, He will give you the strength to climb it. You see, God's grace and mercy will be sufficient in your life's journey, and He will see you through your mountain experiences, even when they are overwhelming. The Bible tells us that by faith we should speak to the things that are standing in our way.

Many of the mountains in our lives are also stress-related, and we all deal with them in one way or another. In our daily mountain climb in life, many people do not even know that they are climbing a stressful mountain until they reach a boiling point.

What is important is not to get to a boiling point, where you let off explosive steam and fire like an erupting volcano from a mountaintop. Remember, what you do and say during your stress boiling point will become the things that you will regret later or for a lifetime.

"Men and women build monuments and structures with their hands and then destroy them with their mouths."

Dealing with life's mountains is important, whether you are in a work environment, home or family, school, or a relationship. You must first determine what your mountain stressors are to operate in the subject environment and cope with your stressors, develop ways to manage the adverse effects of your stress mountains. Sometimes the stress mountains create emotional and psychological states that prevent us from being able to realize our real purpose and direction.

This is because we are living in a perpetually changing world which has made life more difficult to navigate and adjust to. Everyday changes, ambiguity, doubts about the future, and dealing with problems, relationships, crises, and our fears and desires become our mountains. In pursuing your purpose and direction in life, the mountains before you will test your strength, faith, and your belief in God. Your mountains and valleys are a test of your faith and perseverance when faced with the problems in everyday life.

Stress Mountains

Your stress mountain might be your daily task of family or parenting, work, school, money, finances, business, or relationships. Stress is a normal part of our lives, and everyone experiences it in one way or another. It just differs from one person to another.

For example, one person missing an airline flight for a business trip may get angry, while another person may just book another flight and sit down and use this time to catch up on some reading.

Do not get me wrong, some stress is good for us. It helps us sharpen our minds and prepares us to handle life's daily situations, and it may be just a short-term stress effect. Many of us will experience short-term stress effects daily and we recover immediately, but some stressful moments will last a lifetime. The short-term stress effects can be daunting. I will share with you one of my life's interesting short-term stress mountains.

So follow along with me on this journey. Early one September morning after getting off the Metro train at the Farragut West Metro Station in Washington, DC, on Seventeenth Street, I started my morning walk several blocks down to the White House where I worked. The weather was very nice, and because of the impending fall weather, the leaves on the trees were beginning to turn a beautiful, burnt, bright orange color. I love the fall weather in Washington. This time of year, normally the streets would be crowded and bustling with people and cars on any given week's workday as federal and contract workers hustle up and down the Washington streets.

This morning was one of my very early report times for a special White House project, and the streets were empty. So I was enjoying the quietness and beauty, walking down Seventeenth Street without the crowds and the sound of the cars and buses. There was also the pleasant aroma of coffee brewing from the nearby coffee shops on both sides of the street. What was unique on this day was that there was one person, a young lady, directly in front of me, walking to the sounds of her black high heels hitting the concrete sidewalk. To this day I can still remember the dress that she was wearing and the clicking sounds that her shoes made on the sidewalk. The young lady had on a black dress with designs of leaves that matched the surrounding burnt, bright orange leaves falling from the trees lining Seventeenth Street. Life will throw a wrench into your machinery on occasion, but I had no idea that this would be one of these occasions. What happened next was enough to create a stress mountain for anyone. Within a second the young lady in front of me stopped, dropped her pocketbook to the sidewalk, yanked off the black dress, and threw it into the air. The dress floated down directly into my hands in slow motion, leaving me standing there and holding her dress, shocked and breathless.

MARION DEVOE SR.

When this happened, my immediate thoughts were, maybe this was a *Candid Camera* or *America's Funniest Home Videos* episode, so I smiled and looked around to try and find the cameras...But the *Candid Camera* television show had gone off the air many years before.

And *America's Funniest Home Videos* aren't made with hidden cameras. Here I was, six feet, eight inches, a Black man standing on Seventeenth Street, one block from the White House, holding a White lady's dress, and she was standing in front of me half-naked, with only her bra and panties on. My whole life flashed before me, and I could see in my mind a swarm of DC policemen stopping, getting out of their cars, and beating me to death, while the entire event is run on the six o'clock evening news, and everyone would see me as another Black man "falling victim to police mishap."

Now, my first reaction was to run for my life, but I had the lady's dress as evidence in my hands. So I decided to be calm. I asked the young lady to please put the dress back on. She said no. What made the whole thing so eerie was that on this day, there was no usual heavy traffic or people walking down Seventeenth Street, and there was no one for several blocks to come to my aid. I thought to myself, Is this a dream, a nightmare, or perhaps I am sleepwalking? I finally snapped back to reality and asked the young lady again to put her dress back on. She said no again, because a cicada bug was in her dress. Well, the cicadas blanketed the DC Metro area that September in the billions. They were flying everywhere. The cicadas come out every seventeen years in their millions, covering trees, getting in ladies' hair…they are a complete nuisance. The cicadas are about one-and-a-half inches long with red beady eyes; they fly, poorly, into everything and everybody. They were like locusts flying and destroying crops.

Meanwhile, I did not care about the cicadas. My freedom and life were on the line. So with the dress as evidence, and still in my hands, I decided to shake it out, turn it inside out, while the young lady stood there, clad in a pair of black panties with a matching bra, watching me. After shaking the dress out a couple of times, I was able to convince her to put her dress back on. The young lady picked up her pocketbook, thanked me, and walked away as though nothing had ever happened. This was a short-term stress effect that I will never forget.

I, too, proceeded toward my office, but I changed sidewalks, just in case the young lady was ambushed by cicadas again. When I got to my office that morning, I sat down to replay the scene in my head, to make sure I was not dreaming. By then, my secretary came in and said, "Good morning, Mr. Devoe," looked at me and said, "Mr. Devoe, you look like you've seen a ghost." I said, "Yes, I did." She replied, "You see, I told you when we hired you that there are ghosts in the White House and now you can believe me." She had no idea what I experienced that morning, and I never told her the truth. A few minutes later my office phone rang, and it was the White House Secret Service. When I picked up the phone, I could hear laughter in the background. They said, "We saw you on the security cameras on Seventeenth Street and witnessed the entire incident. In the event the DC police came on the scene, we would have come out to cover and save you." They continued to laugh while my heart was still thumping in my chest. They said, "Sorry Mr. Devoe," and hung up, still laughing.

This was one "short stress effect mountain" I will remember for a lifetime. I smiled and said to myself, *At least I was on the Secret Service security cameras and not on Candid Camera*, and I will just keep on climbing my mountains in life.

Race-Inflicted Stress Mountains

Stress can be inflicted upon you in more than one way. I believe that race-inflicted stresses are mountains. The results of America's hate groups, political extremism, and White Nationalism culminate in America's systemic racism. This type of stress can be daunting and is the result of intentional and conscious efforts from others. Today in America racism tends to be covert in nature, and many people may not recognize their actions as being racist acts. Their behavior does not appear to match the more overt forms of racism commonly seen during America's Black Codes and Jim Crow era, when laws stifled economic, political, and social gains by Blacks after Reconstruction. To me, racism is a social construct created by man to legitimize inequality and to elevate one group of people over another group, in order to maintain power and economic advantages—which leads to stress and an abundance of other social problems. When defining racism, some people get *prejudice* and *discrimination* mixed up with *racism*. But they are different: prejudice is prejudgment about others based on some perceived notions and one's background. And discrimination is not racism because discrimination is an action and the result of prejudices. I define racism as the combination of prejudices and discrimination backed by a political and judicial system. This type of racism has created a paternalistic governing system in America and is ruled by tribalism.

Throughout much of American history, many Americans have generally enjoyed legally or socially sanctioned privileges and rights which have been denied to members of various ethnic or other minority groups at various times in America's history.

In America today there are no "privilege safety nets" for everyone, so many people are forced to deal with the racist mountains in their daily lives without any alternatives. So my advice to you is always to be prepared for a slippery slope in your life. America's racism against various ethnic or minority groups has existed in the United States since the colonial era, shadowing many minorities with generations of hate and disparities. People of color, in particular, have faced restrictions on their political, social, and economic freedoms throughout much of United States history and were subject to lynch mobs and massacres, leaving blood stains across America. Even when African Americans were separated in their communities and thriving, White mobs descended upon them and burned and killed them by the hundreds and destroyed their properties. Today in America there is no enactment of Black Codes, public Jim Crow laws, peonage, convict leasing, or lynching mobs. But there are still massacres of Blacks and other people of color by other means. Therefore there is still a modern-day lynching, subtle by the silence, and the conscious intent of blind-eye elected officials, judicial entities, blue uniforms, and other public officials looking the other way and limiting the rights of people of color. This lack of action is steady bloodstaining America's future and dimming the beacon lights of democracy in one of the greatest nations on earth.

The manifestations of hate, greed, power, White supremacy, and racism from the past hundred years are being handed down from generation to generation, creating mountains of destructions and hate across this country.

The hateful practices are ongoing and are casting shadows on minorities throughout America again and again, and there appears no end in sight. We have come to be a country where people of power and advantage are trampling on the one document that serves all Americans, which is America's Constitution. This sacred document is still withstanding the test of time but is now facing the evils of our political extremism. External to the people's turmoil and evilness, there are race reconciliation groups that are actively trying to heal the broken promise of freedom and justice for all in a divisive nation and are making progress with America's efforts on race relations and against political extremism and hate groups.

Often I hear mainstream media talks about the United States being on the verge of another civil war. When I think back to my high school history classes, the truth is, the original United States Civil War never ended. Its laws and philosophy continue into our modern-day society. As a matter of fact, the phrase *civil war* has become increasingly common on the tongues of the far right.

Today in the United States, modern-day America's civil war is not men shooting and killing each other on battlefields.

The modern-day civil war is the rejection of the legitimacy of America's presidential election and the threat to our democracy. The original Civil War didn't start out as a civil war at all; it began when the party that lost the presidential election to the candidate backed by the majority of the country, refused to accept the results of that election. Now, this was over a century and a half ago. So now you can see why I say the original civil war never ended, because this is happening again today in America. In order to properly appreciate the moment that we're in now, we need to understand that, over the course of 157 years, the Confederates and their descendants have really never stopped fighting a war, have regularly and repeatedly resisted and rejected the legitimacy of governmental attempts to establish multiracial democracy in America. This gave birth to White Nationalism and other hate groups. The continuous civil war can be felt today in the form of voter suppression, election deniers, new discriminatory laws, domestic terrorism, the Ku Klux Klan, Proud Boys, Oath Keepers, and other hate groups. I believe to become "one nation under God," on the other side of the mountain, we must put the original Civil War to rest.

> *Put your sword back into its place, for all those who take up the sword shall perish by the sword.* (Matthew 26:52–53)

Interestingly there is another great system and institution that African Americans are dealing with today, which is the one institution that helped and saved many African Americans during the darkest times of America's history. That institution is the African American church.

The African American churches throughout most of America's history were the pillars of faith and hope and encouragement for the communities of people of color. They were united on a common front, fighting for justice and the rights of all people during the civil rights era and saving souls. The African American churches during the era of civil rights were led by some of the greatest theologians and true shepherds of God, and they worked tirelessly and gave many people hope when they had no hope and nothing but despair. These great theologians brought many people together and provided shelter and refuge from the storms during this darkest period of America's history. And yes, these great theologians were true shepherds of God and gave those seeking help a direction in life. Many big and small African American churches were unified and communicated with the communities and shared limited resources

THE OTHER SIDE OF THE MOUNTAIN

for their survival. Many church parishioners found love, hope, and appreciation through these great spiritual institutions.

These great theologians led many African Americans and people of color to the voting booth by helping them to register to vote, thus creating a change movement across America.

Unfortunately, over the years, some of these great spiritual institutions have become eroded and victimized, politicized, polarized by selfish faith leaders, street preachers, and soapbox pastors, falling victim to an autocratic style of leadership, and causing terrible damage to these great spiritual institutions.

> *Jesus said, "I am the good shepherd; the good shepherd lays down His life for the sheep. I am the good shepherd, and I know My own, and My own know Me, even as the Father knows Me and I know the Father, and I lay down My life for the sheep."* (John 10:11,14–15)

I define autocratic leadership style as a dictatorial, domineering, tyrannical, and bossy leadership motivated by control, power, greed, and self, and rarely accepting advice from other church members.

These leaders seek absolute control over everything and everybody in the churches. Today some of these church faith leaders are called pastors, but they are not true shepherds of God. They have drifted toward immorality because of inherited power and greed and the concept of self only. And just like autocratic leaders and dictators throughout the world's history, the church under these types of leaders will eventually fail. Today, across America, these great spiritual institutions are decaying, and some are closing their doors forever.

The central focus of some of these great spiritual institutions now is centered more on church hierarchy, individualism, self-branding, showmanship, money, power, greed, and external political interest, events not related to churches and the Bible.

Many of these churches' leaders are preaching and singing about prosperity and everything except the gospel of Jesus Christ and saving souls.

In reality, some African American church leaders have become myopic in their approach to leading their congregations and today are not focused on their parishioners and the problems that they are facing in everyday life. This non-biblical approach by some church leaders and street preachers lead them far from being shepherds of God.

I compare some of these church leaders and pastors, ministers today in the African American churches, to the bandits and robbers in the Valley of Shadow and Death because they are not the true shepherds leading their flock/parishioners. They are indeed bandits and robbers and thieves standing in front of the pulpit, robbing the congregation of God.

It is my opinion that true shepherds of God are selfless leaders, whereas the bullying autocratic church leaders are selfish, only interested in themselves at the expense of others. What I see happening in some of the African American churches is spiritual abusers leveraging their position of religious authority as faith leaders, thus hurting church members who are seeking God's kingdom.

Such abuse of authority involves a harmful and destructive pattern of leadership that diverts power away from the body of the church for its personal use at the expense of the church members.

When spiritual leaders in African American or White churches are not held *accountable* for their actions, they will impose their will in ways that go far beyond the sphere of control. In such cases these immoral leaders will start to remove those around them who oppose their self-centered power and greedy attitudes. These spiritual abusers will then surround themselves with "yes people" to further their agendas and abuse of power.

> *Do nothing from selfish ambition or conceit, but in humility count others more significant than yourselves.* (Philippians 2:3)

Fortunately, within some of these polarized institutions, there are still some great African American church leaders: women and men of the cloth who deserve credit and who are true shepherds of God. I have been blessed with one of these great leaders at the church which I attend. On the other hand, some men and women of the cloth are just wearing the cloth, and they all will have a reserved seat and accommodation in hell. My prayer is, *I am praying that God will have mercy on their souls and remove the desires from the hearts of the*

immoral church faith leaders from the furnaces of hell so that they may,
too, become true men and women of God and not of Satan. Amen.

> *Churches are a place where evil should flee*
> *but have become a refuge for evil.*

2

LIFE'S MOUNTAIN EXPERIENCE

◇◇◇◇◇◇◇◇◇◇◇◇◇◇◇◇◇◇◇◇◇◇◇◇◇◇◇

IN WRITING THIS book, my stories are seen through my life's lens of the actual living history of mountains and valleys, highs and lows, experienced in my lifetime that I have witnessed across America. As an African American male growing up in the South, my grandfather was a positive role model for me many years ago. I heard and witnessed many of the horrific stories from my grandfather about his generation and the generation before him growing up in the South, and the threats of lynching and stories about angry White mobs stringing up Black men to trees as an act of hate, violence, and power. According to my grandfather, the acts of violence were to maintain White supremacy and power for the economic, social, and political systems in the deep South. I learned early on that the hateful mountain spirit from Whites has been around for years. It has proliferated even in modern-day America into our political, legal, social, and economic systems. I will share with you some of my mountain climbing stories while growing up in a community blanketed by racial hate and disparagement. I grew up in Savannah, Georgia: a beautiful port city with a dark history of racism, still one of the largest ports in the country. But the port city's historic claim to fame was this: this port was the South's primary point of entry for ships arriving full of slaves, as cargo from West Africa, on every lower-level deck of the ships.

Over two hundred years ago, the warehouses lining the famous tourist district, Savannah's River Street, were filled with cotton and enslaved families. Some have said that you can still see the marks and remnants on the walls where slaves were chained as they waited to be sold and auctioned as property.

Families were torn apart, and men and women wept as they were separated from their families and sold on auction blocks. They would never see each other again. Many perished and died from the harsh labor and treatment of their slave owners.

Many older Savannahians have said that the Savannah city's gothic Victorian houses are haunted by ghosts from the past inhuman practices; these leave an eerie, chilling feeling on tourists as they tour beautiful Savannah's historic district.

Through the years growing up in Savannah, I, too, witnessed my parents and other adults in the community where I lived endure mountains of inhuman treatment and racial hate handed down upon them by Whites.

The most troubling incident I can recall as a young child was on one occasion when my grandfather took me on a day labor trip with him to pick cotton.

Perhaps then child labor laws did not apply to day laborers and cotton fields, or just were ignored by the employers seeking cheap laborers. Regardless of the situational institutions, I enjoyed bonding with my grandfather as a child. The day labor trucks often would pick up the laborers from my neighborhood early in the morning, before sunrise, at the end of the street where we lived. The truck used to pick us up was a flatbed truck fashioned and modified to carry as many laborers as possible. It had a canvas top supported by two-by-fours fashioned in a box shape to cover the truck's payload. On the insides and under the canvas cover, there were three long, wooden benches the length of the interior of the truck, without back support. When I think about the truck now, the interior design mirrored the lower decks of slave ships and was designed to be packed full, just like the slave ships, with day laborers for long, hot days in the sun to pick cotton. We all boarded the truck and, of course, my grandfather kept me close to him. We got into the canvas-covered truck and sat on the hard wooden benches, one by one, destined for the cotton field to pick cotton. In my mind, I pictured slaves doing this without pay.

While the truck was en route, it was traveling through the dark back roads of rural Georgia's forbidden places—forbidden for Blacks to travel alone during this period. There was a man on the truck nicknamed "Piccolo" who I would often see in my community standing on the street corners playing the harmonica. I never asked my grandfather why they called him "Piccolo" even though he played the harmonica, not a piccolo, out of respect for my elders. As the truck traveled down the road and as we all sat tightly together on the wooden benches, I watched each person transition into a state of mind to prepare themselves for the long, hot day in the sun to pick cotton for wages that were close to nothing. Now to help us all get prepared mentally for the day of labor, Piccolo played a sweet song I believe was "Summertime," a 1933 song composed by George Gershwin for the opera *Porgy and Bess*, which lulled me to sleep as I leaned on my grandfather's shoulder. I was suddenly awoken by a loud boom as my grandfather pulled me close to him. The tire on the right rear of the truck carrying us to the cotton field blew out. The driver of the truck pulled over to the side of a rural road in pitch blackness. I could hear the engine of the truck coming to a complete stop as the driver turned it off. Then I heard the sound of the truck door opening followed by the footsteps coming toward the back of the truck. To me, as a child, this was like a horror movie, hearing footsteps coming toward us in the back of the truck in the pitch darkness.

But then a bright light appeared on our faces as the man from the passenger seat stood in the back of the truck shining the flashlight over us. We were all seated on the three rows of wooden benches, and as I looked around, I could see fear in the eyes of each laborer as the man with the flashlight asked one of the men on the truck to get out and change the tire. One elderly man on the truck complied.

We all filed out of the truck and stood on the dark, rural Georgia roadside as the elderly man changed the truck tire in the darkness under the dim light of a flashlight. One unique thing about the African American subculture is that we tend to use an abundance of nicknames for each other in certain geographical areas of the country. The nickname of the elderly man changing the tires was "Switchblade." I asked my grandfather why they called him Switchblade and he said, "The reason why they called him Switchblade was because he carried a long pearl-handled switchblade knife."

When Switchblade finished changing the tire, we all got back in the truck one by one and were seated on the hard wooden benches for the long ride to the cotton field. But when Switchblade started to get back inside the truck, the White man with the flashlight called him back out and said, "Boy, next time don't take so long to change a tire," and slapped him in the face so hard it echoed into the truck as we all watched in vain. And there was nothing we could have done to aid him because of being in the middle of nowhere in rural Georgia.

Switchblade got back in the truck and cried and said, "If I was on the streets of Savannah, I would have killed him, but not here, because it would have put us all in danger." As he continued crying, some of the women and men sitting next to him on the end of the bench tried to comfort him, while Piccolo started playing the song

"Summertime" again to help change the mood. We were all shocked by what just happened. What I found out later was that Switchblade had spent twenty years in prison for killing a man during a gambling game and was out on probation, and his only source of work was as a day laborer because no one would hire him. After all, he was a convicted felon. Many years later, I asked my grandfather whatever happened to Switchblade and he said, "Switchblade went back to prison and is serving a life sentence for killing another man who called him a 'boy' while boarding a city bus downtown in Savannah." Sadly, this was an example of a painful climb up a hate mountain in this man's life, who became a victim of his circumstances. When the truck reached the cotton field, we all unloaded and lined up to receive the burlap sacks and burlap sheets to be filled with cotton.

I watched each person take a sack and align themselves with what appeared to me to be an endless row of cotton, to begin the long, hot day. We picked the pure white cotton perched on three-foot-tall brown stems, each having several bolls of cotton (lint or fibers). As for me, I trailed my grandfather step by step, and I picked the lower bolls of cotton as my grandfather swiftly pulled the cotton from each boll and placed it in the burlap sack over his shoulders. Finally, at the end of the first row about a mile down the field, my grandfather started another row of cotton. I trailed him, picking the lower bolls as he was moving down the row at an immeasurably high speed, picking the cotton. I did not understand the method back then, but many years later, I learned that the cotton had very little weight and that each person would need a lot of cotton to earn money because each laborer was paid for the amount of weight of the cotton at the end of the day. By the time my grandfather reached the end point on the second row of cotton, we were back at the starting point. At this point, my grandfather emptied the burlap sack filled with cotton onto the collection burlap sheet for weighing at the end of the day. My grandfather usually was very talkative but said very little on this day to me and just smiled at me as he kept humming some song that I could never figure out. I knew the incident that happened on our way to the cotton field that morning had disturbed him and the others that day, and many of them will never forget it.

At the end of the day in the sweltering sun, each laborer would stand by their filled-up burlap sheets and wait for the cotton field owners to come by and weigh their cotton for pay.

At this point, each laborer received their pay. When they got to my grandfather's collected cotton, he had the largest collection of cotton picked that day.

However, when they weighed his burlap sheet, which was larger than that of the person next to his, the cotton field owners issued the same weight as the others. My grandfather said, "Hell no," that this is not the same. These were words from him I never heard before. I watched the silence between the cotton field owners and my grandfather, and I feared for my grandfather, but the field owners walked away and came back and gave my grandfather the correct weight and money that he earned that day. After this horrible day, and witnessing the early morning slapping incident, my grandfather never took me on another day labor trip. As per the opera song by George Gershwin, "living in the South was not easy."

> *This poor man cried out, and the Lord heard him, and saved him out of all his troubles.* (Psalm 34:6, NKJV)

The conceptualization of racism in America today is the result of being influenced by others. Some people tend to form their own opinions, beliefs, and views, and simply just hate others for no real reason. I have lived long enough and witnessed enough of America's acts of racism to understand this. This practice is not healthy for our society and country today, and it is the reason why we have continuous turmoil in our cities, counties, the federal government, and political and judicial systems. I have come to believe that not all people who grew up in families and communities where racism was the norm become racist people. On the other hand, some people have hate and prejudice in their hearts and will continue this behavior and wave their flags of divisiveness throughout America with their racist conspiracy theories and lies upon lies in hopes of influencing our political, social, and economic systems of governing. This hateful approach is a recipe for the destruction of democracy and a precursor for violence in America. I believe that America's racism is a default key for Americans who hate people of color. The main danger America is facing today as a country is the continued coexistence of racism and democracy. The fabric of our country and what it was created on is now being shredded and trampled by political extremists. Our founding fathers established rights for all people, but these rights are being taken away and eliminated from the one doctrine that was enshrined with liberty and justice for all.

No Mountains Are Too High for God

The most insidious thing about ascending man-made mountains, regardless of the type of mountains they are, is that they are designed for you to eventually fall off a cliff into pits of disparities, segregating you with no way out. I am not by any means an expert on actual mountain climbing, but in my comparison of earthly mountains to the man-made mountains of our construct, I can add some climbing instructions.

First, natural mountains were created in time to withstand time, and only God can move mountains. So the idea of eliminating the mountains of man will be an endless battle. When climbing your earthly mountain in life, your goal is to avoid the evils of man by bridging a path/route around the evils and continuing your climb up your mountain. No mountains are too high for God. I know this for sure because when I moved to the Washington, DC, area for a position within the US Postal Service HQ, I faced many evil mountains of man. I thought I had made it and was living the American dream, and then the mountain of man appeared before me. I moved my family into my first single-family home in Northern Virginia in a quiet cul-de-sac area. My kids were very young then, and my wife and I kept them on a close watch because of being new to the area. My neighbors were nice to my knowledge, but one evening after arriving home from work, I saw them gathering in the cul-de-sac, so I walked over just to say hello. They were engaged in a conversation, so I decided to join them as well. As I approached them, one of the neighbors caught my eye as I was approaching and gestured to the others to disperse.

They quickly ended the conversation, and each went back into their houses and left me standing there. What I later learned was that there were a couple of burglaries in the community, and they suspected me and my family of being the culprits. This felt awful, and of course, was a form of prejudice; after all, mine was one of the only two Black families in the entire neighborhood then. Had I remembered the concept of racism, I would have been better prepared for the outcome of my move to a predominately White neighborhood. The basic concept that I grew up under was, "stay within your own Black neighborhood," and out of an all-White community. But Northern Virginia was the home of many military and government workers living in diverse communities, and I thought that my family being Black would not matter. So this was a rude awakening and a reminder that I was still Black. No matter where I moved the basic concept of racism would follow me. In other words, you cannot outrun racism. Throughout my life, a Shepherd watched over and protected me and my family. Yes, God has a way of showing people their mistakes. It was discovered by the neighbors that the burglaries were committed by teenagers who lived completely outside of our neighborhood. There were never any apologies from my neighbors. "Only God can change and move mountains." Your mountains in life come down to the decisions that you make also, whether to climb it or just let it stand and walk away.

So when faced with mountains, think positively, and this will help you climb up and actuate your optimism.

Whatever mountain you are facing in life right now that leaves you breathless and your mind shouting for help to abandon the climb, rather than giving in and giving up, I suggest you stop a moment and take a deep breath, and look at where you need to go in life. I know the task feels daunting and there are a thousand reasons why it would be easier for you just to give up and even abandon your faith. But before you give in to your despair, I want you to look back to see how far God has brought you and at the steps that He brought you through to where you are today. Whether there were large strides or little steps, they required effort on your part. But you did it anyway and you never gave up. Remember, God was right there to help you, and He'll continue to help you, so never give up, and just keep climbing.

Men run away from a stressful situation in life's
pursuits, but God runs toward man.

God did not create man to hate one another,
this is an acquired behavior of man.

As we journey through life, we will learn to adapt to the stresses around us as we climb the mountains. Some obstacles and mountains will be easy; others may be more complicated.

Remember no mountains are too high for our God.

Whenever you come across a mountain too high to climb, you must remember to not only focus on your inner strength for your mountain climbing, but you must focus on the one who created earth's mountains for your strength: God.

Be Encouraged

To overcome your mountains in life, you should name your mountains and take them to God for help. You can probably imagine the names I have for the mountains in my life. So when I encounter people's mountains, I simply ask God to clear my path away from them. As a Christian I know that not all people are good for you; some pose a problem for you and your life.

Like most people, there were many mountains in my life before me, and it was through God's Grace and mercy that I overcame my mountains.

I have asked myself several times how was it possible for a poor Black child from Savannah, Georgia, living in a house with an "outhouse," one generation outside of segregation, the first of ten children to graduate from college, to make it up to Washington, DC, and work at the White House. It was through God's grace and mercy. So, in your despairing moments in life's journey, and as you are climbing your mountains, no matter what the situation is, remember that God will be there for you, and he will take you up the mountains and will not abandon you in the valleys of your life.

3

RELATIONSHIP MOUNTAINS

◇◇◇◇◇◇◇◇◇◇◇◇◇◇◇◇◇◇◇◇◇◇◇◇◇◇◇

YOUR MOUNTAIN CAN negatively impact relationships, whether it is a work relationship, with friends, family/marriage, or other personal relationships. Remember, your first goal is to decide what is the "stressor" impacting your life in your relationship. Let's first look at some of the relationship's stress mountains.

Broken Relationships

Too many relationships with the wrong people will lead you off a cliff. I have witnessed many people over the years, young and old, trying to fix a broken relationship. I have also seen the misery and pain in many relationships. I have concluded that a relationship cannot be mended once it's broken, no matter what you do to repair it. When you do try to mend it, this will only prolong the hurt and heartache and pain in your life. I do realize it is hard to move on from a broken relationship and let go, but one must face the facts when one has been climbing a relationship mountain day and night and getting nowhere. Every day you put all of your strength and efforts into a relationship and still it gets you nowhere.

When you wake up each morning and look into the mirror, you can see the misery lining your face. This misery is like a cloud of rain that follows you all day, and people can see it.

But stop and think: have you tried God? So when you are on a slippery slope, this is the time to find another mountain to climb and place your trust in God, and He'll help you reach your peaks in life and descend the mountains and take the path through the valleys to a happier life. I know some people say they are in love, but love is not always enough to make a relationship last.

First, love stands for more than just a romantic attraction, sex, or strong feelings toward those close to you; it also stands for truth, trust, respect, security, commitment, and godliness.

When God places you back on your feet, after a broken relationship, stay away from those who knocked you down.

Lack of Respect for Relationships

Respect to me is defined as your deep admiration for someone or something within one's heart. To me, a lack of respect is no regard for someone or something dear to you or others. So lack of respect and respect are mutually exclusive. For example, I had two neighbors who lacked respect for others, including respect for their spouses and my spouse, and they both were at least ten years senior to me.

Back then I lived in a very nice neighborhood with houses neatly lining the concrete streets. The only problem was the houses were built too close to each other. I will not name the locations where I lived during the sinful encounters and lack of respect mountains in my life then.

One neighbor on the left side of my house, who I called the "no-respect lady," came over early one morning after hearing my newborn son crying as I was preparing his milk. That morning my dear wife had prepared my son's milk and set it up before departing for work. My neighbor, the no-respect lady, knew my wife was gone and so was her husband, so she decided to try her sinful mountain climb with me. She came over and rang my doorbell, and I went to the door and there was my neighbor, all clad in a pink negligee, standing there smelling and drenched with perfume, saying, "Can I help you with the baby?" as she opened up her negligee and smiled. I was speechless and shocked, but as a man of faith, I said, "No and thank you" to the no-respect lady. Then the sinful nature of man in me came out and I lied. I said that my wife went to the store and was on her way back and should be pulling up any minute now. The smile on the lady's face disappeared as she quickly jumped off my porch and scrambled back across my front lawn—she took the shortcut back to her front door by leaping across the hedges that separated our properties, leaving a plume of perfume floating in the air.

After hurdling the hedges like a track star, she tripped and landed face down in her flower bed. Now her husband had green thumbs, and in each growing season he would load up his beautiful flower beds with horse and cow manure for the growing season.

I heard her screech when her face got buried in the manure, as I watched her through my bedroom window. She quickly got up, spitting out bits of horse and cow manure, and the negligee she was wearing was no longer all pink. It was speckled brown and black. I heard her front door slam as she went back into her house and the sounds of swearing spewing out of her mouth.

The no-respect lady knew right from wrong, but she did her sinful deed anyway and paid the consequences, through retribution theology, in the well-manured flower beds because of her lack of respect for others. This was a relationship mountain in my life then, and fortunately, the lady never came back to my house again. But occasionally, I would see her getting in her car in the mornings when I was taking out the trash. She would drive by and give me the finger; I would just simply smile back and then laugh. I believe respect for each other should be mutually agreeable in a relationship. If you have respect for yourself and others, you will have a loving and happy relationship as you climb your relationship mountain.

Ungodly Relationships

Now on the right side of my home, there was another neighbor, who I would always see smoking a cigarette and watching me through her kitchen window as I cut my lawn. I describe her as ungodly and called her the "ungodly lady mountain." Being a former athlete, I enjoyed staying in shape, so I took up running to tone up my physique. One sweltering summer morning I went for my usual three-mile run. When I returned, due to the heat, I took off my shirt and I decided to wash my car before it got too hot. In the car mirror, I noticed my neighbor watching me while I was washing my car. The neighbor on the right side of my house, the ungodly lady mountain came outside. Smoking a cigarette, she said, "Good morning, there."

I replied by saying good morning and continued washing my car. She walked up to the rear of my car and placed her right foot on the bumper, then slowly raised her dress up her leg so that I could see what she wanted me to see. I was shocked.

The ungodly lady mountain then said, "Are those shorts you got on too hot? Come inside my house and take them off and let me dry your body off," and then winked at me.

Again, being a Christian man, I said no to the ungodly lady mountain and continued washing my car.

She took a puff on her cigarette and said, "Are you sure?" By then, my dog sitting in the shade under a tree in my backyard had had enough and began to growl at her and slowly stalked toward her. As my dog got closer and started barking at her, she took off running and ran out of one of her house shoes with my dog on her trail. I called off my dog. My dog came back with her house shoe in his mouth and took it back to his shade spot and begin to chew it up as the ungodly lady mountain continued to watch me through her kitchen window. When I was finished washing my car, she was still watching me through her kitchen window and still smoking a cigarette.

I simply waved at her as I was going back into my house, and of course, she gave me the finger. I just smiled and went into my house. In both of the scenarios that I have mentioned, I averted a potential moral compromise by maintaining my boundaries to avoid the sinful pitfalls of mountains.

I must say that it was many years after I moved away that I told my lovely wife about the sinful mountain incidents, and as humorous as this was to me, my wife did not see the humor in it but did smile.

Climbing a sinful and tempting mountain will lead you to your demise.

Over the years I have seen many of my friends and coworkers seeking out greener pastures or other relationship mountains, just like the ones I have mentioned above, but they soon realized that if they had tended to their pastures, their pastures would have been greener. This myopic attitude and approach have destroyed many relationships, marriages, and families.

Belligerent Relationships

The belligerent relations mountains are provocative or combative. They will argue about almost anything, almost anywhere, regardless of the situation. Here is one I observed while taking the Metro to work one morning. On my way to work, I grabbed a morning paper, as I usually did to pass the time as the Metro train traveled to Washington, DC. Once the train arrived at East Falls Church, Virginia Metro stop, which was still several stops away from mine, a couple got on the train and sat directly across from me. There was nothing unusual about the couple boarding the train that morning.

Normally I watch everyone boarding the train as a precaution, for safety in my commute to and from work daily. I kept reading the newspaper. The couple started talking, as most people do, as small talk just to pass the time while riding the Metro train. Soon this conversation turned into an argument. I kept reading my paper and ignored the argument between the two. But suddenly the man arguing with the young lady yelled out to me, and said, "Mister, tell this woman that I am right." I hated his tone of voice and the lack of respect for the young lady, but I looked up in a perplexed manner and said nothing. The man then said again, "Sir, please tell this [expletive] woman she is wrong." By then I had had enough of his belligerent attitude and did the only thing possible to ignore them. I dropped my paper into my lap and pointed to my ears, to describe that I was deaf and could not hear, and pointed to my mouth, meaning that I could not talk either.

The man, in a spitting rage, yelled at the woman so loud that everyone on the train turned to look. The man then said to the woman, "You see you got me talking to a deaf mute," and he continued to belittle her and use profanity. When the train got to the next stop, it was a relief for me and the other passengers when they both got off. But I could see them still arguing as they walked on the station platform. What was so humorous about this mountain experience was the lady sitting adjacent to me, touching my shoulder and gesturing to say, *Sir, I am so sorry they bothered you.* I said, "No, I am sorry that I had to pretend to be deaf." The lady said, "You can talk and hear?" I said, "Yes, I just like to keep out of other people's problems," and we both started laughing. This couple on the train that I encountered was a perfect example of an ill-fated relationship mountain, a couple heading for a cliff. I later prayed for the young lady that day, that she would soon realize she was in a bellicose and unhealthy relationship. In my opinion the relationship was too far beyond what counseling could repair or save. Only God can move mountains. What I am saying here and throughout the chapters in this book is that we all have mountains in our lives casting shadows, creating doubt, fears, and storms in our lives, and flooding the valleys of our minds with pain and hardships. It is only with God's help that we can overcome these mountains.

> *Let all that you do be done with love.* (1 Corinthians 16: 14)

In your relationship do everything out of love. Arguing, for instance: do it out of love because you care so much for that person. This is because God does everything for us with love. When in doubt pray to God about your relationship mountain.

I once met a couple on a Zoom call for a marriage seminar. Each married couple had an opportunity to share points concerning marriage and conflicts. One couple said that shortly after their marriage and before they were able to relocate and share the same household, they lived in separate states. Their relationship was solid; however, when they had a conversation, it sometimes turned into an argument. Now the man was a minister, and the woman was an attorney. When they started to argue, the husband knew that his chances of winning an argument with his attorney wife were zero, so the husband would always start the conversation with a prayer. And of course, I know of no one who can argue with someone praying. So always pray during your relationship mountain disagreements.

> *Love suffers long and is kind; love does not envy; love does not parade itself, is not puffed up; does not behave rudely, does not seek its own, is not provoked, thinks no evil; does not rejoice in iniquity, but rejoices in the truth; bears all things, believes all things, hopes all things, endures all things. Love never fails.*
> (1 Corinthians 13: 4–8, NKJV)

Love should not hurt; love is not jealous; love does not hate; love is not angry; and love is not mean. Love is not your definition because God has defined what true love is. He will hear your cry for help.

God is always here for you, and He is always here to help strengthen you in your relationship at the bottom of the mountain, or the top of the mountain, or in the valleys of your life.

People have often asked me how to make it in a relationship and marriage, and I would often tell them to use my quote: "If you make her/him happy, she/he will make you happy," and there is an opposite side to this as well, "If you make her/him unhappy, she/he will make you unhappy."

I have heard some people in a relationship saying, "I am waiting for him/her to get their act together." I have often said to them, is this a Broadway show or a movie production? In other words, in movies, actors portray make-believe characters and have the opportunity to film a scene over and over again until they get their acts right and together. No one should have to live their lives like this and wait for someone to get their act together. Your relationship should be a real-life situation and not make-believe.

In this situation it is time to close the curtains on this show and throw away the movie script, turn the television off, or walk out of that bad-rated movie. Simply tell your actor/actress that you live in the real world, not on a movie production set, and the show is over.

Contemptuous Relationship

These are hurtful, disrespectful comments aimed at the person, such as put-downs, which are often some form of superiority, said with the intention of distancing themselves. In this case the person uses an insulting statement to make their point. For example, the person may ask you to do something and then say, "That is the least you can do." This is what I call intentional insults.

Domineering Relationship

They are the controllers of everything. They are in charge of all aspects of your life. In this case you will feel like you have another parent over you. They are the "do this or that" relationship people and are always giving orders. This will also be prevalent when you are out in public. In life each mountain has a boundary, so set boundaries in this type of relationship. Let others know when they exceed your boundaries and that they are out of bounds for your tolerance in the relationship.

Relationship Experiments

People tend to want to create and change a person to be what they want so the relationship will yield their desired outcome. Take this for an example: one of God's unique creatures is the zebra. It is so fascinating with its unusual black and white stripes. Some people may want to experiment and paint a zebra all black or all white and call them horses. In reality no matter what colors you paint them, they are still zebras. Going into a relationship in hopes of changing someone is an experiment. God did not create you in His image as an experiment. Genesis 1:27 states: "So God created mankind in his own image, in the image of God he created them; male and female he created them." So do not take on a relationship for a lifetime as an experiment in hopes of changing a person to your desired outcome. For women: "He is the total of all the riches on earth, and you have the key to his treasures." For men: "She is the total of all precious jewels on earth, and you are her soulmate and the guard over her treasures."

Mistakes and Bad Decisions

Some people wonder why relationships sometimes simply do not work out. They start by saying they made a mistake by going into the relationship. People often use the word *mistake* to cover up for bad decisions they have made. Mistakes are something you do without intention—for example, turning down the wrong street.

Bad decisions are conscious intents made without regard for the consequences or the outcome. For example, going into an unhealthy relationship when you know the outcome will be failure, stress, and pain. But many people do it anyway. It is easy to dismiss your bad decisions by calling them mistakes. In other words, going into a troubled relationship, when you know from the beginning that the relationship will cause you heartaches and pain, is a bad decision. Don't let your unwise decision cause you to ignore injurious behavior, abuse, red flags, and fools. No matter how attractive you are to the other person, "never fall for fool's love, because fool's love is like fool's gold, which is nothing but a worthless piece of stone." If you are in a relationship, think about how much it matters to feel heard, valued, and understood by the other person in the relationship. Having someone who understands and values you is being in a true relationship. This is the result of communication between the two involved in the relationship. Notice I never mentioned three or four persons in the relationship, if you get my point.

Men: "Remember, if you treat her like a queen, you will become her king."

Women: "If you treat him like a king, he will become your king."

Relationship Success

The success of relationships between people is the result of mutual feelings and attraction for each other. On the flip side, without these attractions, it will be hard to foster positive and loving relationships in your life. The relationship can be stressful and has the potential for distance and disagreements and disconnection between the ones you care about. Sadly the stress in relationships increases if, when you open your mouth, you communicate negatively. On the other hand, saying nothing will smooth things over for a while, but will eventually bring about another dispute. It is not difficult to "sin in our speech when you open your mouth." I have lived long enough to realize that only spiritually mature people can control their tongues.

> *If anyone among you thinks he is religious, and does not bridle his tongue but deceives his own heart, this one's religion is useless.* (James 1:26, NKJV)

> *For we all stumble in many things. If anyone does not stumble in word, he is a perfect man, able also to bridle the whole body.* (James 3:2, ESV)

> *But no man can tame the tongue. It is an unruly evil, full of deadly poison. With it we bless our God and Father, and with it we curse men, who have been made in the similitude of God. Out of the same mouth proceed blessing and cursing. My brethren, these things ought not to be so.* (James 3:8–10)

A person's tongue can tell a lot about that person, just like when you go to a doctor and the doctor asks you to open your mouth to examine your tongue, which tells him whether you have a temperature, digestive problems, or another health diagnosis. The doctor can tell just by examining the coating on your tongue.

> *Remember, in life, your tongue will tell people a lot about you when you open your mouth.*

Communication in Relationships

Many people say communication is the key to a healthy relationship. But I conclude that this is an aberration because lying is a form of communication and so is yelling, which is prevalent in a lot of relationships. You can build a relationship on truth, but lying will destroy what you built.

Don't get me wrong, I do believe in sound communication within a relationship, but communication is not the only foundation of a sound relationship. Trust is the foundation of a solid relationship, and without trust there will be no relationship.

Security in a Relationship

When it comes to security, men and women define security differently. For example, some women see security as emotional support, while some men see security as financial support. As a man, I see security as being both financial and emotional support in a relationship. In a relationship with emotional and financial support, no mountain will be too high.

Walking with God

Remember, God took you up the mountain and He will take you down into the valleys of your life, and surely, He will not abandon you there in your relationship. Think of the darkest times in your life when you were dealing with uncertainties and problems; you had no strength to go on and people turned their backs on you. Each day when you woke up your tears washed your face, and your body felt heavy because of the hurt, pain, and grief you carried inside. God took control, lightened your load, shined His light upon you, and brightened your day. He wiped away your tears, and He carried you up and over the mountains in your life. God will not abandon you in the valleys of your life as well.

When walking through the valleys of life, walk with God, for He will lead you on to your destination in life.

When you walk with man, you will only be going for a walk, and man will lead you to your demise.

> *Yea, though I walk through the valley of the shadow of death, I will fear no evil: for thou art with me; thy rod and thy staff they comfort me.* (Psalms 23:4)

I can reflect on my own life when my daughter Jordanne Devoe was at the University of California (UCLA). As she was finishing her climb up the academic mountain and approaching graduation, "the dark valleys" appeared before her and fear set in. She started to worry about her final exams and how to prepare for them. She called me on her cell phone for advice and for strategy for studying for her final exams.

Being the dad that I am, I tried to discuss ways of preparing for the exam that she was so stressed about, but I couldn't get a word in the conversation because of her venting. I still tried to calm her down. While we were on the phone talking, she suddenly stopped and said, "Dad, I got to go; I can't find my cell phone." I said calmly, "OK, Jordanne, call me back when you find your cell phone." She then realized that she was talking to me on her cell phone. We both laughed. She did graduate from UCLA, even with the dark valleys that came along with it, and she has learned to deal with valleys in her life. She now is a fashion designer and has her own line of women's swimwear: Deveaux Swimwear.

We all have mountains before us, and the mountaintop experience can offer great relief, but then we all must go through the valleys in life.

The problem with humans is that we tend to live in tribes that create mountains in our lives. Because of this we tend to congregate in groups formed by our ideologies, party belief systems, and race. Now, tribes demand loyalty, and with loyalty comes membership and protection and separation from other tribes, by any means possible. Within America's tribalism, the winning tribes take all and push their agenda down on the losing tribe. When this continues to happen, eventually the winning tribe's domination over the losing tribe will lead to the self-destruction of the dominant tribe from within.

4

The Mountain-
Climbing Instructor

◇◇

WHAT INSPIRED ME to author this book was *not* all the events that are happening in our country and around the world today. It was an unusual event that occurred in my life while riding the Metro train to work one day in Washington, DC. During this time I had some storms in my life. I was confused about my direction, and my doubts and my fears were taking over. On this day, during one of my many commutes to work, I met an elderly man whom I saw walking slowly toward the Metro train one morning as I was boarding.

The elderly man was well dressed, wearing a navy blue pinstripe suit—one of my favorite work choices because navy blue or black suits seem to be the required attire for White House staff. The elderly man also wore a light blue paisley necktie with a white cufflink shirt.

He was wearing black shoes with a high shine, and he carried a weird, brown leather saddlebag as a briefcase, with initials in gold,

G. A.—one like I have never seen before. He was a slim-built Black man with a neatly trimmed hairstyle.

He and I got on the train at the same time, and he sat directly next to me that morning. I said, "Good morning," and he replied, saying, "Good morning, young man." I took out my usual morning paper, starting my daily reading to pass the time, and the elderly man looked down and said, "What are you reading about, young man?" I politely said, "Sir, nothing much; I normally read the papers to pass time on my commute."

This is when the wisdom from the elderly man poured out. He said, "Son, there is not much in the newspapers these days except bad news. You should want to hear and read about good news, and rarely are you going to find it in the newspapers." He said, "You see, son, the papers make their money by spewing bad news about people and the economy daily as they journey up the mountain in life." He then said, "Isn't this why they call it 'daily news' and laugh?" I politely listened, even though I disagreed with him. The one thing that interested me most and stuck with me was his analogy of life being a mountain to climb, and this is what inspired me to write this book. The elderly man said, "Life is a mountain to climb, young man, and you start at birth and you just keep climbing throughout your life.

"Your parent teaches you the basic climbing skills, and then everyone you encounter thereafter builds on this. You start your life-long journey with the challenging task of climbing up the mountains of life.

"Along the way you will meet several people doing the same thing and taking on the same task of climbing up, just like you.

"Unfortunately, some people you will meet climbing will not make it to the top and will just fall off a cliff to their demise."

I thought to myself, What a horrible prognostication to share!

To me, this morning, the ride to Washington seemed like it took forever. The train car was moving, rocking back and forth along the tracks as I listened to the elderly gentleman. It seemed like time stood still, and I heard no other sounds or voices on the train that morning except the voice of the elderly man.

He went on to say that during your journey up the mountain don't worry about the path or trail behind you, just focus on what is in front of you and keep climbing.

I said very little as he kept talking and talking. He then proceeded to talk about descending the mountain, down into the valleys of life, but then he said this will be the darkest time in your life and when the real troubles start. I said, "Sir, isn't this when things should be better?"

He abruptly stopped me and said, "No, no, young man, you see this is when the enemies will come at you more strongly. Why? Because you have made it to the other side of the mountain and descended into the valleys of life." The elderly man quoted this scripture, from Psalms 23:1–6: "Yea, though I walk through the valley of the shadow of death, I will fear no evil: for thou art with me; thy rod and thy staff, they comfort me."

As the train was slowly approaching my stop, I said, "Sir, thanks for the advice. This is my stop—and have a wonderful day." The elderly man just smiled and waved me off and then clutched his leather saddlebag as though he had completed his mission.

I got off the train and I turned around to wave goodbye to the elderly man, but when I looked toward the area where we were sitting, the seat was empty.

I immediately thought, Perhaps he walked toward the rear of the train and got off at the rear exit—but no one exited the rear door. I thought to myself, I don't know his name or where he worked, and this was my first time seeing him on the train.

I stopped and thought, Did I drift off to sleep while reading the newspaper, was I dreaming, or was the elderly man an angel? I walked toward the Metro station exit wondering what had happened to the elderly man sitting next to me.

I will never know, but deep in my mind I believe God placed an angel in my path to advise me on the journeys ahead of me in my life and to lead me through the valleys of my life.

Since then, I fear not because I know that God is with me every step of the way as I journey through my life's valleys. The next morning on my commute to work, and thereafter, I looked for the elderly man, and I never saw him again. As I have stated, I believe he was an angel from God.

I thought about it further: that morning when I encountered the elderly man in the Metro station parking lot, I did not see him get out of a car. The elderly man just appeared out of no-where, like magic.

As I remembered, the Metro station's parking lot was full, and I took the last parking space in the entire parking lot. When the elderly man trailed me through the Metro-card entrance, he never swiped a Metro card or inserted a card or money. He just waved an empty hand and the gate opened as he walked through—like magic as well.

When I glanced over at him, he walked side by side with me and took the same number of steps as I did, and even turned when I turned, just like my shadow following me on a sunny day.

I found this so amazing. How this all happened, after I put all the pieces together—I know some would have been frightened by this incident I have illustrated, but to me, this was a wonderful occasion. Since then, I know God watches over me as He does for you, so have no fear, for "Thou art with me," step by step, as Psalms 23:1–6 says. God is real! I am a witness to this.

I am sharing this with you because this was not the only time in my life that I have encountered the mere presence and the power of God.

If you will just stop and think, there were times in your life when you encountered something similar and experienced the existence and the presence of God in your life as you climbed your mountains, so have no fear, for God is with you always.

When you are facing mountains in your life, He will provide you with a mountain-climbing instructor.

5

WORRYING MOUNTAINS

◇◇

> *Do not be anxious about anything, but in every situation, by prayer and petition, with thanksgiving, present your requests to God. And the peace of God, which transcends all understanding, will guard your hearts and your minds in Christ Jesus.* (Philippians 4:6–7, NIV)

WORRY HAPPENS WITHIN your mind; then it is relayed to your body in the form of stress. In the valley of worrying, people tend to worry about things that have not even happened, or are things out of their control, about which they can do nothing. Worrying so much can become a heavy burden, weighing negatively on your health, relationships, self-esteem, career, and other aspects of your personal life. It can also impact you physically, emotionally, and mentally, contributing to the mountain you must climb. Worrying can leave imprints on your mind, and in some cases, change your facial expression.

MARION DEVOE SR.

I remember 1969 when I got drafted into the military only a few days after finishing high school, and later after my basic advanced training, when I received orders to go to Vietnam. As a young man, I watched my mother cry as I departed on my very first-ever airplane flight destined for the Vietnam war.

When I left home, my mother was a vibrant, youthful-looking woman, even after giving birth to ten children. She was only thirty-nine years old at that time. When I returned from Vietnam thirteen months later, I saw firsthand what worrying had done to her. She looked like she had not slept a night since I departed. Her eyes were all puffy and her facial expression had changed and hardened; she looked to be in her early fifties. When I walked up to her and hugged her, I cried not only because I was finally home, but because I saw how the worrying and the burden and concerns for me had caused her to age by ten years. Many years later in one of our many conversations, she told me that she worried about me being killed in Vietnam and prayed for my safety. She had cried every night while I was in Vietnam. God answered her prayers and protected me. This was a dark time in my mother's life and my life, but we managed to climb that mountain with the help of God. So when you consider worrying all the time, consider also the damages it may cause to you and those around you. Remember, worrying is our own construct and a man-made mountain; casting shadows; creating doubt, fears, and storms in our lives; and flooding the valleys of our minds with pain and hardships. It's natural to worry about what is happening or about an upcoming event in your life. But it is excessive when it's persistent and uncontrollable. You worry every day about "what-ifs" and worst-case scenarios. If you can't get anxious thoughts out of your head, they will interfere with your daily life.

Worrying and Fear

You must ask yourself, Where is my faith? Constant worrying, negative thinking, and always expecting the worst can take a toll on your emotional and physical health and will create a mountain in your life because of your fears. It can take away your energy and emotional strength, leave you feeling restless and jumpy, cause insomnia, headaches, stomach problems, and muscle tension, and make it difficult to concentrate at work or school. Worrying can also be a common mountain in your life that involves tension, nervousness, and a general feeling of unease that changes your whole life. Worrying is in your mind, and its force can be broken by thinking positively and looking at life's reality and being less fearful.

> *When you lie down at night, you will not be afraid, your sleep will be sweet.* (Proverbs 3:24)

I have met many people over the years who fear life in general. They worry about almost everything and are afraid of flying on an airplane or even riding in the front seat of a car. They fear the days and they fear the nights and even God's rain. When asked about their fears, none of them had ever experienced a traumatic event on an airplane or been involved in a serious auto accident to warrant these worries and fears. Their worrying was due to a lack of faith.

I define their lack of faith as having no trust or confidence in God's ability to save or protect them.

I respected their dysfunctional belief systems and their fears, but I still encouraged them to trust God and not worry.

> *Fear not, for I am with you; Be not dismayed, for I am your God. I will strengthen you, yes, I will help you, I will uphold you with My righteous right hand.* (Isaiah 41:10, NKJV)

Worrying can also lead to mistrust in others. Take this for example: a person is all alone on an elevator when it stops on a floor, and another person gets on who looks different from them. Their first reaction is to worry for their own safety—when in reality, the person who got on the elevator has no interest in them and is focused on their own business.

> *For God hath not given us the spirit of fear, but of power, and of love, and of a sound mind.* (2 Timothy 1:7, KJV)

When you worry it's tough to be productive in your daily activities, and worrying controls your thoughts and will distract you from work, relationships, and life. Do not worry about all the stuff going on in your mind or all the reasons that you think you should not be happy.

Those things you think are bad or terrible often turn out to be nothing great overall. Get rid of as much of the unnecessary stuff in your mind that is troubling you as possible. Remember the enjoyable times that made you happy and you will smile each time. Live your life each day. Life is too short to worry about the unimportant things that you have little or no control over. I remember going to a small neighborhood church with my grandfather as a child before my mother moved us away from my abusive father.

During the church service, there was a song that the choir always sang during the altar call for prayers: "The Lord Will Make a Way Somehow" by Thomas Dorsey. This song stuck in my mind for a reason, later on, that year after we moved away from my father.

My mother moved the family across town, trying to make it on her own, and struggled financially with five children then. I was the oldest boy, around six years old.

One night just before bed, I walked past my mother's room and saw her sitting on the side of the bed in the dimly lit room, staring at the ceiling. I walked in and said, "Mom, what is wrong?" And she said, "Son, I'm all right, and I got a lot on my mind." I knew she was worrying. Being a child, I did not know how to comfort my mother. But I remembered that song from my grandfather's church and I said, "Mom, the Lord will make a way somehow." She looked at me as her eyes filled up with tears. She tried but could not hold back the tears and started crying. All of my other siblings heard her crying and came in, and we all hugged her. My mother had faith in God, but the mountains before her were huge during this stage of her life. She had a doubt that she could make it on her own then with five children.

Worry and doubt will make it difficult when we are trying to overcome the mountains in our life. Faith and doubt cannot occupy the same mountain. Worrying weakens our faith. My mother's worrying did not solve her problems, but it brought her comfort from the ones she loved most.

With her strong faith in God, she prevailed. Even going back to my abusive father and having five more kids, she never stopped praising God for all his blessings in her life as she journeyed up and down the mountains and through the valleys in her life.

Unplugging Worrying

Another cause of worrying today is the use of technology, which intensifies our worrying and the mountains before us. We are physically and mentally plugged into technology like cell phones, computers, and iPads, and all the apps on them, which are overloading our minds with things to worry about.

We are consumed with the postings on Facebook and Twitter, which will eventually raise our stress levels.

The most logical way to de-stress is to literally unplug yourself from the technology around you. When you are spending too much of your time looking at a phone screen or sitting at a computer desk, it's easy to cloud your mind with all the events around the world today, creating fears and doubt and cutting off the ones you love and cherish most.

Taking time out of your day to unplug from your devices and enjoy those around you will strengthen your relationships with your family and God. Remember, modern-day technology and the rapid news media and television are creating more mountains in our lives.

What makes matters worse with these modern technological devices is that we often will try to predict the future outcome of current events, sporting events, elections, stocks, investments, and other events happening in our lives. But it does not always happen as we predict. Thinking about all the things that could go wrong does not make life any better. Focusing on worst-case scenarios will only keep you from enjoying the good things you have in the present and your current life situation. You can plan for tomorrow, but live your life for today and leave tomorrow up to God.

> *So do not worry about tomorrow; for tomorrow will take care of itself. Each day has enough troubles of its own.* (Matthew 6:34)

It is OK to think about the future and plan for the future because this is strategic planning. Planning things out reduces stress. On the other hand, worrying is not strategic planning. It is speculations, fears, and anxieties about something. When you worry you carry the heavy burdens around with you day and night, and you place your trust in yourself. But when you place your trust in God, He will take your burden and lighten your load.

> *Then Jesus said, "Come to me, all of you who are weary and carry heavy burdens, and I will give you rest. Take my yoke upon you. Let me teach you because I am humble and gentle at heart, and you will find rest for your souls.* (Matthew 11:28–29, NLT)

Stop a minute and think about all the dark times and how you overcame the mountains in your life. It was God who picked you up from the lowest point in your life and placed you back on your feet.

I am here to tell you as a witness that I, too, have been there, and God has lifted me and He has been there for me. And yes, He will be there for you as well.

When it rains in your life and the wind tears at your very soul and no one comes to your aid, God will shelter you from the storms. When you are all alone at night at your darkest hour and you toss and turn in bed about your mountains, God will carry you up them. When your tears from your pains and hurt and disappointments in your life will fill a dry riverbed, God will give you perfect peace, remove your tears, and make a way out of no way for you.

Worrying can take a heavy toll. It can keep you up at night and make you tense and edgy during the day. In most chronic worriers, the anxious thoughts are fueled by the negative and positive mountains you face. You may believe that your worrying helps you avoid bad things and prevents problems and troubles. But it's tough to break the worry mountain if you believe that your worrying serves a positive purpose. Once you realize that worrying is the problem and not the solution, you can regain control of your life. It's tough to be productive in your daily life when your worrying is dominating your thoughts and distracting you from work, school, or your home. There will be many mountains and valleys, and you will overcome them; worrying should not be one of them.

You should try to enjoy being on the mountaintop because getting there will be tough, but up on that mountain, it is easy to praise God for your journey. But then life happens, and we will find ourselves no longer on the mountain. Our mountains test our strength and through God, we can make our way up. The valleys will test our faith and question our belief in God. Remember that God will be with you on the mountains, and He will take you through the valleys.

6

APPROACHING THE VALLEYS

◇◇◇◇◇◇◇◇◇◇◇◇◇◇◇◇◇◇◇◇◇◇◇◇◇◇◇◇◇◇◇◇

> *You prepare a table before me in the presence of my enemies; You anoint my head with oil; My cup runs over. Surely goodness and mercy shall follow me all the days of my life, And I will dwell in the house of the Lord forever.* (Psalms 23:5–6, NKJV)

OUR MOUNTAIN EXPERIENCES represented our struggles and desires to move up and the hard times and difficulties that came with it. We all have had great mountaintop experiences: college graduations, loving relationships, marriages, job promotions, the birth of a child, achieving our goals, and seeing our prayers answered. And there have been good times and bad times. God responded to our times of need and struggles, and we made it to the top with His grace and mercy. As inspiring as life's mountains are, though, they don't last forever because circumstances constantly change. You will inevitably start your journey down the mountain and through the valleys to the other side of the mountain.

> *I have told you all this so that you may have peace in me. Here on earth, you will have many trials and sorrows. But take heart, because I have overcome the world.* (John 16:33, NLT)

Be encouraged that on the other side of the mountains our valleys are temporary, and they do have an end. Know that each valley in your life has a purpose. Everyone will go through valleys at some point, and some more than once. *The valley experiences are entirely different from the mountain experiences.*

The valleys do not discriminate, and we all will eventually go through one. Valleys do not take days off. The valleys are inevitable and purposeful. The Bible tells us that the "valley of shadow and death" was the main route that travelers took in their route to Jerusalem: through a deep, dark, shadowed canyon. The surrounding hills and mountains created a dark shadow in the valley. This lack of light created a hiding place for bandits, thieves, and robbers to prey upon travelers on their journey to Jerusalem. To make this journey even worse, if the bandits and robbers did not get them, the wild animals would prey upon the travelers. Our journey in our lives today is similar. While we don't travel through the dark valley of shadow and death in a physical sense, we understand it in a metaphorical sense. Psalm 23 is about walking through "the shadow of death." This is a metaphor for life's trials in general, though it also applies to a person facing his/her death or the death of a loved one. In this life, we face many trials, some of our own and others from God. Our dark valley days might look like our physical suffering and chronic pain, loss of a loved one and sorrow, betrayal, or a valley of haters.

Our valleys could be a troublesome job, the wayward child, the marriage falling apart, jealousy, our finances, our sickness, grief, and our fears. We may also go through valleys of doubt, despair, and even sin and temptations. In all of these valleys, it can feel like we are all alone. We can rest assured that God knows the way through whatever valley we are in. He knows what it feels like and the presence of shadows of death. He knows we will face temptation, doubt, fears, and hate. In our valleys God will be with us every step of the way, even though at times we may have doubts.

> *I am the good shepherd. The good shepherd gives His life for the sheep.* (John 10:11, NKJV)

In our valley journeys, we have a Good Shepherd who went before us and even now leads us and guides us, protecting us during the darkest times in our lives. The valleys are where life becomes challenging and where many battles are fought. They are where feelings are hurt and where our tears flow freely and where we meet God.

> *Faith is not immune to trials; it is fueled by trials.*
> (1 Peter 1: 6–7)

The valleys are where our attitudes are developed and changed and we can see ourselves in the mirror. The valleys are the places where we struggle every day with fears and hopes and painful circumstances.

Our valleys may be spiritual warfare or the actions of others or because of our rebellious actions, hate, or even due to the hands of God Himself for our disobedience. In our mountaintop experience, we go there to experience God's presence, but the valleys are where we find God and He comes to our rescue as we shout out and cry out for His grace and mercy.

Just like in life when there are dark clouds in the skies, there could be dangerous storms coming; so for every mountaintop experience, there will be a dark valley that you will go through. As one of my church pastors would say, "You're either going into a valley or coming out of a valley or amid a valley." In our lifetime there will be many trials and sorrows; there will be people who will misunderstand you; they will criticize you, talk about you behind your back and even lie and betray you. This will be one of the many valley experiences that you will have to go through. Remember that you are not alone in the valleys because you were obedient when you went to the mountaintop to experience the presence of God. Now God will come to you in the darkest hour of your life, and He will see you through your trials and tribulations. We live our lives seeking to get to the mountaintops. But we do not live there always, although we love our mountaintop experiences with God. In general, we spend the greatest amount of our lives in the valleys. Life is tough in the valleys, but there are valuable lessons that we can all learn there that we could never learn if we stayed on the mountaintops.

God has a purpose for every valley that He takes us through.

> *We can rejoice, too, when we run into problems and trials, for we know that they help us develop endurance. And endurance develops strength of character, and character strengthens our confident hope of salvation. And this hope will not lead to disappointment. For we know how dearly God loves us, because he has given us the Holy Spirit to fill our hearts with his love.* (Romans 5:3–5, NLT)

In your life you may have valleys full of doubt, fears, and discouragement. God has a reason behind this, and you will get through your valleys with Him. Everything you go through in life has a purpose, whether big or small: it is to shape us. I know this for sure, being a former athlete, a basketball player. My basketball coach, Edward Jinks, at Tompkins High School (the mighty Wolverines, Savannah, Georgia!) would drill my team over and over for defense and offense plays to build our strength and prepare us to perform on the basketball court to win games. The preparation was successful: during game time we upset one of our biggest rivals, Beach High School. So the valleys in our lives are similar: there we build our strength, endurance, and faith in God. How do you know how much endurance you have unless you have to face tough times? How do you know if you can trust God in challenging times unless you go through them?

> *Yea, though I walk through the valley of the shadow of death, I will fear no evil: for thou art with me; thy rod and thy staff, they comfort me.* (Psalms 23:4, KJV)

The Valley of Fears

Know that God wants to use your valley experiences to strengthen your faith. Remember that God will help you overcome anything that's causing you to fear. Ask God to give you strength in your valley and to walk through fears. Use your time in the valley to learn how to trust God more, knowing that you are not alone during the darkest hours and struggles in the valley of fear.

I have walked through the valley of shadows of death and dealt with my fears. Many years ago, while in combat in Vietnam, I served a tour of duty as a radar operator during the most turbulent years of the war. Vietnam became a killing field for the dreams of young and talented American men and women, those who never lived to fulfill their dreams because they perished on a foreign battlefield.

With God's grace and mercy, I survived the battles, yet my mind and body are broken and torn forever. In Vietnam I was stationed on an outpost overlooking the Demilitarized Zone (DMZ), no-man's-land, an extension of hell on earth. I experienced ground attacks, mortars, and rockets day and night. I witnessed the death of my fellow soldiers—harrowing events that are hard for me to describe even fifty years later, to this day. I witnessed young soldiers on the battlefields dying on the ground after an enemy attack, saying their last words, I want to go home. I can write about this now because time brings about some healing, and with the help of God through His grace and mercy, He made me whole again.

In Vietnam, whenever I would write home, I would write about the good times in the city of Saigon, but in reality, I was not stationed in Saigon. I was stationed in one of the most dangerous combat areas of South Vietnam, some four hundred miles away from the city of Saigon. Every day I was met with the fear of being zipped up in a body bag or blown up to the point of being alive but physically destroyed forever. For my safety I stayed inside the underground bunker operating the radar set and away from enemy sniper fire. But part of my combat mission was a rotational assignment to Dong Hoi Mountain, "the mountain of the shadow death" as it was called by some radar operators, because of the number of fallen operators there and the dark shadow that the mountain cast over the valley. The Dong Hoi radar set was situated on the top of a mountain not far away from the Khe Sanh (pronounced Kay-Son) area of Northwestern Quang Tri Providence, Republic of South Vietnam. This was where, on January 20, 1968, the US Marines were under siege by the North Vietnamese Army (NVA) for days, taking a high number of casualties—but the NVA also took heavy casualties, and in the end, the Marines won the battle There was only one way to get to this outpost on top of Dong Hoi Mountain and that was by helicopter. On the day of my assigned rotation to Dong Hoi Mountain, I received a radio call telling me to be ready at 0600 for a pickup from my outpost location on the DMZ.

When the helicopter arrived that morning, the sun was just rising, and I could see the beautiful sunrise on the horizon as I had never seen it before, and just then my fear set in. At the age of nineteen, I wondered, Could this be the last sunrise that I would ever see on earth? I prayed and asked God, Please do not let this be my last sunrise on earth. On that morning another radar operator and I boarded the helicopter with all of our gear and supplies for the two-week assignment on Dong Hoi Mountain, the place I called "hell on earth" and not the mountain of the shadow of death. The helicopter took off and flew for a while over the beautiful Vietnam terrain near the city of Quang Tri, overlooking Vietnam's villages with their neatly constructed straw houses, built in circles on the ground below us. As we were in flight, there was a feeling of comfort and safety. We were in the cool, morning-fresh air and able to see the beautiful landscape—without looking through a perimeter of barbed wire fence and mine fields, the "chambers of hell." It was a relief not to smell the gunpowder and diesel fuel from the military tanks, and the previous night's ground attack firefights with the enemy. In our low-flying helicopter flight, I could see the Vietnamese tending their rice paddies with the water buffaloes pulling the plows. From above I could see the Vietnamese children gathering on the roadside, waiting for soldiers to drive by on their way to pick up supplies from our rear units. The children gathered on each side of the roadside seeking the soldiers' gifts. After flying for a while, we were approaching Dong Hoi Mountain.

The view as we were approaching the mountain was an amazing sight to see, as though God had painted a mural of the mountain on earth.

It was beautiful to see, yet it was a dangerous mountain nested in the thick of tall, green elephant grass and trees. As we flew in from a distance, there appeared to be a puffy white cloud that covered the mountaintop. The white cloud looked like a giant white cowboy hat sitting on top of a giant green cowboy boot. Isolated in the middle of nowhere, it was a place where no soldier should die. As we were approaching Dong Hoi Mountain, I could hear the chopping sound of the helicopter blades that echoed off the mountain as we flew nearby. When the helicopter reached the foot of Dong Hoi Mountain, the pilot hovered over a wavering field of tall elephant grass; the turbulence of the fast-spinning helicopter blades pressed the elephant grass down for our freefall jump. The pilot then yelled back at us, "Due to enemy sniper fire I could not land on the mountaintop." He then said he would hover at the foot of the mountain and we would need to jump out. To clear the area for our jump, the door gunner on the helicopter then rolled his M-50 machine gun around and let off a burst of about a hundred rounds of fifty-caliber bullets for any would-be enemies waiting on the ground for our jump. The M-50 gun's bullets fired by the door gunner were so powerful, they completely chopped up the tall elephant grass like a giant lawn-mower. One can only imagine what this powerful weapon does to a human being.

The pilot then said, "Prepare to jump," and I grabbed my weapon and gear and walked through the smell of gunpowder from the smoking M-50 gun and I jumped out of the helicopter from a roof-top height.

The free-fall jump and the fear that came with made it feel like I was in the air forever, but it was only for a few seconds. I was holding my weapon tight, ready to fire if I needed to keep from being killed. I landed in the elephant grass, which cushioned my fall without an incident. When I looked up at the helicopter still hovering above, the other radar operator was still standing at the helicopter's door, holding on for dear life. But then he received a shove from the door gunner, who pushed him out and threw our supplies out with him. I could hear the radar operator's expletives as he fell toward me. He landed on his back in the elephant grass, but instead of grabbing his gear, he grabbed his weapon and pointed it at the helicopter as though to shoot it down. Fortunately, he did not even have a magazine clip inserted in the weapon. It did not matter anyway; the helicopter was gone in a matter of seconds after our freefall drop. I trusted God, but I had let my fears kick in and place doubt in my mind that God would protect me. When we doubt God's protection, fear will set in and we will lose all hope. The other radar operator and I gathered our gear and started our climb up the mountain. Just like today, when we fell down, we had to get up...and just keep on climbing up the mountain.

As we climbed, there was a neat path cut through the thick, lush, tall green grass. This was cut by US Army engineers to hide us from enemies. On our climb we not only had to worry about enemies, but there were also venomous snakes: one bite would kill you if you were not medevacked immediately. The mountain was so steep that we could only climb a few feet at a time in the 120-degree heat, carrying supplies and weapons. Climbing a steep mountain was not only very dangerous in itself, but at any point an enemy could pop out and engage us in a close hand-to-hand combat attack. In comparison, in our everyday life, we have enemies every day that try to derail our every move, just like the band of robbers and thieves in the valley of shadow and death. My advice to you is to keep your focus on the one who created the mountains and valleys, God, to protect you. God will protect you in your mountain climb and He will protect you in your valley journey. Remember, whatever mountain or valley you are on or in, God is your Shepherd and promises to be with you every step of the way.

> *Yea, though I walk through the valley of the shadow of death, I will fear no evil: for thou art with me; thy rod and thy staff, they comfort me.* (Psalms 23:4)

This scripture phrase that describes, "I will fear no evil: for thou are with me; thy rod and staff will comfort me" illustrates that the Shepherd that herds the sheep carries a rod and staff as he reigns over the herd of sheep. The Shepherd used the rod and staff to lead the sheep to greener pastures and guide the sheep that strayed away from the herd back to the herd. Likewise, God is our Shepherd, and He, too, reigns over us as our Shepherd; He, too, carries a staff and rod to guard and protect us and lead us as we stray away from Him through the valleys in our lives.

In my valley of fear, God led me through the dark valleys, and although I struggled with my fear, He kept and protected me in the darkest hours of shadows and death. I am sharing this actual valley of fear story because our valleys can be beautiful and dangerous at the same time.

There is a distinct difference in purpose, yet they both apply to God in our lives. I overcame my valley of fear with the help of God, and I know that you can too. In the valley of fear, your only enemy is fear.

The metaphoric mountains in our lives are a test of our belief in God and the valleys are a test of the strength of our faith.

The Valley of Storms and Rain

The metaphoric storms you go through in life are to test the strength of your faith. The Bible illustrates this in Mark 4:35–40 (NKJV).

This vivid illustration describes an event in the life of Jesus, the son of God.

> On the same day, when evening had come, He said to them, "Let us cross over to the other side."
> Now when they had left the multitude, they took Him along in the boat as He was. And other little boats were also with Him. And a great windstorm arose, and the waves beat into the boat so that it was already filling. But He was in the stern, asleep on a pillow. And they awoke Him and said to Him, "Teacher, do You not care that we are perishing?" Then He arose and rebuked the wind, and said to the sea, "Peace, be still!" And the wind ceased and there was a great calm. But He said to them, "Why are you so fearful? How is it that you have no faith?"

You see, the storms in our lives are not meant to destroy us but to turn us toward God. We become apathetic until we face a severe storm. There will be many storms in your life, even the one you are facing today. They may include the loss of a job, a health crisis, loss of a business, loss of a loved one, or financial downturns and hardships. Many of us will struggle in our valleys of storms. It is because we are trying to walk through our valley alone. God often brings storms into our lives to shift the focus from ourselves and our lives to Him.

For comparison, while I was in Vietnam during the heavy monsoon season in 1969, being a young soldier, I woke up early one morning after my radar operation shift and decided to go for a mail run, some sixty-nine miles in the rear to pick up mail for my unit on a road called "sniper and mine alley" (SMA) because of enemy sniper fire and land mines.

During the rainy season in Vietnam, many soldiers would often say "the only difference between hell and Vietnam is the rain."

I jumped in my company's Jeep and headed out of the gate for the treacherous and dangerous ride down a long and winding, muddy, red clay road. In the blowing, blinding rain hammering the Jeep's windshield, the stricken wiper blades struggled to keep pace. I drove about three miles and decided to turn around, due to the blinding, blowing rain, and return to my outpost, Charlie-two on the DMZ. As I made a U-turn on the narrow muddy road, another army Jeep with three soldiers honked at me, yelling, "Get out of the way," and sped off down the slippery road in the monsoon rain. I made my U-turn, returned to my radar site, and told my fellow soldiers that the road and weather conditions were too treacherous for me to continue to make the mail run. Within an hour, sadly, I received a radio call that the Jeep that passed me on the muddy road hit an enemy land mine that killed all three of the soldiers in the Jeep. This was another horrible loss of young soldiers in Vietnam that I will never forget. But in my case, God sent a gust of blowing, blinding rain at me and turned me around, and I was obedient, which saved my life. I am here today to share this story. In our everyday lives, there are consequences for our disobedience and rewards for obedience. God uses His metaphoric storms and rain in our lives every day to turn us around also, so be obedient and you will be rewarded. As you struggle through a storm today, keep in mind that God is watching over you and He is with you every step of the way, so be encouraged and be obedient.

Remember to trust God as you weather your life's storms, no matter how rough and painful they are. God will help you through it all. Storms are scary and we tend to panic. So don't panic during your valley of storms; no matter how much it rains in your life or how loud the thunder or how sharp the lightning strikes or your suffering, trust God during your valley of storms. You see, some storms and rain are to wash away the things in your life you don't need.

God is more powerful than any storms you could ever experience in your life's valleys of storms and rain.

The Valley of Suffering

This valley could be uncomfortable, painful, and tearful, and you may suffer at some point. That loss of a loved one, the child that rebelled, the business that is going south, and the marriage falling apart. We have all these things in the valley of suffering that are things we have to get past.

The mountain is no longer the place of praise, and valleys are now where we are standing. Know that God won't allow you to suffer any more than you can bear and that the suffering He allows you to experience is all for a good purpose. Use your time of valley suffering to get to know God and love Him more and trust Him more. Don't lose your heart during your valley of suffering because, in the end, this will result in a more positive you. Be encouraged; the valleys of suffering don't last forever.

The Valley of Direction

While walking through your valley of direction, don't let yourself become disoriented in your darkness. Stay focused on God, His light. Some people would say to focus on the light at the end of the tunnel. But I have come to believe that this light could be coming from a fast-moving train. So focus on God because He is the light. Be assured that even when your circumstances confuse you, God knows what He's doing in your life and has a purpose for your directions and every one of us. It's always easier to focus on God when things are going well, but we sometimes forget God when things are going south until we are heading for a cliff, and then we shout, "Lord help me!" The point I am making here is to stay focused on God and let Him lead and guide you. I learned one interesting lesson about staying focused, while growing up in Savannah, Georgia. I remember, as a young child, watching my grandfather, and the many lessons of wisdom I learned from him.

Now my grandfather was a railroad retiree who became some-what of a farmer in the neighborhood where we lived after he re-tired from the railroad, and he would plow fields for various other neighbors in preparation for the growing season. He would always pick me to go along with him on his daily field-plowing jobs, on his wagon pulled by a horse. On one occasion, while I sat under a tree in the cool shade, eating an apple, watching my grandfather calling out commands to his horse named Nellie, I learned all about the importance of staying focused.

I watched my grandfather and Nellie strategically plowing the field, turning the black, rich soil over in neat rows in a straight line for one of our neighbors. On this day about midway through the field, for some reason, Nellie came to a complete stop and refused to move or follow my grandfather's commands and calls. I could hear my grandfather saying, "Giddy up Nellie, giddy up," in his Geechee dialect. But Nellie never moved an inch and just stood there like a statue of a horse. Frustrated, my grandfather came over to where I was sitting in the shade and got a bucket of cool water and some sugar cubes. But even after Nellie siphoned up the fresh water through her pursed lips and ate the sugar cubes like they were chocolate, she reverted to being a horse statue.

Being a young child who loved to watch cartoons on our small black-and-white television at home, I remembered a cartoon about someone using a stick, tied to the horse's harness with a carrot dan-gling in front of the horse's eyes, as a way to encourage the horse to keep going. So I said, "Grandpa, try using an apple tied to a stick hanging in front of Nellie's eyes. Maybe she'll move on down the field pulling the plow." My grandfather's eyes lit up, and he said OK and did just as I suggested, using the last apple we had as part of our lunch.

Nellie started plowing just as before and kept up plowing as she stayed focused on the apple. Row by row my grandfather guided Nellie down the field, yelling out directions and commands. But there was a distinct difference in Nellie's direction and focus now. Nellie was motivated by the dangling apple in front of her eyes. She just kept moving forward, focused on the apple. My grandfather struggled to hold on to the plow as perspiration was beading up on his forehead. He had to make sharper turns because Nellie's eyes were focused on the apple and nothing else.

On the very last row of plowing, I watched as all hell broke loose as my grandfather and Nellie were approaching the end. I heard my grandfather say, "Whoa Nellie, whoa, whoa, Nellie!" That horse kept her eyes focused on the apple, tied to the string on the stick attached to her harness. She just kept going, ignoring my grandfather's commands.

My grandfather started using some expletives I never heard from him before (being a church-going man) as he pulled back on the plow with all of his strength. Nellie was approaching a railroad track separating the plowed field from a two-lane highway with fast-moving cars coming from both directions. His efforts proved useless. I saw the plow snap into two parts as Nellie crossed the railroad track, and the plow blade hit the first rail. Fortunately, there was no train coming on the track.

By then my poor grandfather only had Nellie's reins in his hands to try to stop Nellie from being hit by the cars on the highway. Nellie went into the street as though no cars were coming. I could hear cars slamming on brakes as Nellie crossed over the two lanes of the highway and headed into the adjacent woods with my grandfather holding to the reins for dear life, still shouting, "Whoa Nellie, whoa Nellie!" I could see from a distance people getting out of their cars to try to come to the aid of the poor old man, all clad in his old blue denim coveralls with a red handkerchief hanging and flapping in the wind from his rear pocket, trying in vain to bring Nellie to a stop. As for me, I never left my shaded spot under the tree as my grandfather had given me specific instructions not to leave it. But I could see from a distance what happened as Nellie came to a complete stop in the woods.

The apple, still dangling from the stick in front of Nellie's eyes, got hit by a tree branch, and Nellie was able to pin the apple up against a tree. Nellie rewarded herself by eating the apple.

I could see my grandfather stroking Nellie's head gently as he untied the stick and pulled Nellie directly by the harness to guide her back across the street safely.

My poor grandfather was able to bring Nellie back to where I was sitting. My grandfather's blue denim coveralls looked like he had gone for a swim in them; they were so soaked in sweat from the whole ordeal of my cartoon suggestion.

My grandfather hooked up Nellie to his wagon, picked up the fractured plow, and put it at the back, and said, "Climb on board, son, and sit next to me." After I climbed on and sat proudly next to my grandfather, he said, "Giddy up Nellie," and we rode off down the road, heading home as though nothing happened. When we next went plowing, my grandfather never packed apples in our lunch again. What I learned from this encounter with an apple and a horse was that Nellie stayed focused on the apple and nothing else. So in our valley of direction, we should focus on God for our directions and not get distracted or disoriented by others. Stay focused on what is in front of you, and God will lead you to the apples of your life.

> *My son, keep my words and treasure up my commandments with you; keep my commandments and live; keep my teaching as the apple of your eye.* (Proverbs 7:1–2)

The Valley of Uncertainty

The valley of uncertainty is deep and painful; it waits to ambush you. It knows you're coming. It waits around the corner for you. And once it has you in its grip, it does not want to let you go. It is like the bands of thieves and robbers lurking in the darkness in the valley of shadows and death. It never takes a day off and it does not discriminate.

It's like a long-term bad relationship; it loves you to stay for a long time. It is like a road filled with holes and bumps, stretching for miles with no end in sight. And it makes it hard for you to leave because it grips your mind. It helps you look for someone or something to blame for why you're in this state of uncertainty. It specializes in blaming others. And it loves putting questions and doubts in your mind that you have no answers to. Uncertainty can fill our lives and confuse our thinking process. God knows and guides our future. We make uncertain plans late at night for tomorrow, and while we are asleep, God smiles at our plans and fixes them.

> *A man's heart plans his way, but the LORD directs his steps.* (Proverbs 16:9, NKJV)

The valley of uncertainty is the master of doubt.

When life feels uncertain, it's easy to doubt that God is really with us. But the God who is with us during the good times is the same God who is with us during the bad and uncertain times. He doesn't abandon us. Be assured that God is with you now while reading this passage. *God is our refuge and strength and is always ready to help in times of trouble and uncertainties. We should not fear when the dark clouds appear in our lives and storms come our way because God will help us through the valleys of uncertainty.*

Be encouraged, let go of your control, and let God take control. It is most important to trust God during your valley of uncertainty. God is our anchor and the firm foundation when the storms of life are raging all around us. God alone knows and guides the future. Live your life one day at a time and enjoy every minute of it as best as you can. Praise God for giving you your life, and ask Him to walk with you through your dark valley of uncertainty. The valley of uncertainty you are in now won't give you the answers or the directions to your life. Your valley of uncertainty will only keep you from being where you want to be in life. The one thing that you should ascertain is that God is real and He is certainly by your side and will lead you out of your valley of uncertainty today and tomorrow.

> *God is our refuge and strength, a very present help in trouble.* (Psalms 46:1, NKJV)

The Valley of Discouragement

During the valley of discouragement, take advice from people whom you trust and who are close to God, rather than those who won't encourage you. The valley of discouragement is painful, and it hurts because you feel you cannot go on. When we are in the valley of discouragement, we lose our passion and purpose in life and have no courage to go on. The valley of discouragement is like the fishermen that cast their nets all night and came up with empty nets, as Luke 5 describes. Your valley of discouragement is only keeping you back.

Take your problems and pains to God, and ask Him to empower you to handle them according to His will. Ask God for encouragement and know that He will give it to you. When you are struggling with discouragement, you need to assert your trust in God. When we find ourselves in the valley of discouragement, we sometimes turn to man. Well, man will not encourage you, but will only lead you to more wilderness. We also turn inward on ourselves with self-pity. Having a self-pity party will not lift you out of the valley of discouragement. Know that discouragement and disappointment are normal emotions in our lives, and we all will experience them at times. I know this for sure because I, too, have been faced with many discouraging moments in my life. Despite my persistent prayers and my desires, things did not always turn out the way I wanted them to. There were times when I became angry with God for my disappointments, and I felt that God had abandoned me in my times of need.

These were the times of struggle in my life, and my dreams were taken away by things I had no control over, like being drafted into the military, destined for a war in Vietnam only six days after graduating from high school.

What I have learned from my valley of discouragement is that what I wanted was not in God's will for me then, during this particular time in my life. There was a bigger and better plan for me, and I had to go through this valley to make it to where I am today. God has a strategic plan for all of us. I was not prepared mentally, physically, psychologically, and spiritually for the path that God had for me. I needed to climb the toughest mountain and go through several valleys to be able to walk the road in life that God paved for me. I know this for sure, and I can see now and I know that there will still be discouragement. I have learned to trust God and not depend on man and myself. I can now say, "Thank you God for being my Shepherd and my guide through the valleys of discouragement. Halleluiah!"

Valley of Sickness

In our valley of sickness, God will intervene according to His will and restore our health if it is meant to be.

We are of flesh and blood, and illness and sickness will come upon you and cast a dark cloud over you. This is the time to pray to God and ask Him to give you strength and healing. This also applies to your loved ones, so intercede for your loved ones and your medical professionals. Keep praying until answers come. Ask others, especially strong Christians, to pray for you, and let them know your specific prayer requests.

But be careful who you ask to pray for you. I once heard a coworker talking to another coworker and asking her to pray for her recovery from her serious illness. Of course, one can only imagine what she prayed for, since she wanted the lady's husband. Choose wisely who you want to pray for you. Don't wait for others to contact you; take the initiative to contact them. Seek the best medical care you can find and pray and never give up.

7

THE VALLEY OF BETRAYAL

◇◇◇◇◇◇◇◇◇◇◇◇◇◇◇◇◇◇◇◇◇◇◇◇◇◇◇

THE VALLEY OF betrayal is probably the most devastating loss a person can experience in life. People will betray you for thirty pieces of silver as they did Jesus (Matthew 26:15). The valley of betrayal is like a beautiful magnolia tree in your front yard that produces white, sweet-smelling flowers every year which you love to see, but then the tree gets struck by lighting and all the leaves and flowers fall off and all the tree branches die. The tree now becomes an eyesore and ugly to look at when you walk by. So now you hate the sight of it; you cannot stand the sight of the tree anymore. I define betrayal as the act of someone violating your trust, which changes your feelings and attraction to them and you cannot stand to see them anymore, just like the unsightly magnolia tree. This could involve lying to you, abusing you, or someone putting their interest first in a relationship. With the loss of a loved one, you physically lose that person forever. With betrayal, you lose that trust forever, even though God says we must forgive. The reason why the valley of betrayal is most devastating is that most often it is a loss that occurred because of the conscious intent of someone else.

During your valley of betrayal, you will be overwhelmed with emotions, unable to overcome them. You may want to inflict harm on the person who hurt you, to hurt them as deeply and as excruciatingly as you were hurt. But this will only bring you more hurt later.

Every betrayal valley has its own story and its own healing time. Just like the loss of a loved one, something that you will never get over; still, you will learn to live with it.

When you are in your valley of betrayal, ask God to give you peace and comfort, even when you cannot see ahead of your hurt and pain. Ask God to walk with you through your darkest hours of betrayal to calm the storms in your life that are tearing you apart and to bring you peace and sunshine again.

Let God deal with your betrayer. In the valley of betrayal, our inclination is to strike back at the one who hurt us. You should refrain from seeking revenge. We must turn our enemies over to God and allow Him to administer justice.

> *Dear friends, never take revenge. Leave that to the righteous anger of God. For the Scriptures say, "I will take revenge; I will pay them back," says the Lord.* (Romans 12:19, NLT)

The Valley of Jealousy

I believe that one of the most destructive emotions of all is jealousy, which also grows on the tree of betrayal. Jealousy occurs when we look at what others have and think we should have it instead. We become that green-eyed monster. When we are jealous, we are saying that God has not done right by us. We are saying that we know better than He does how our lives should go. This is the time to rejoice for others, but instead, we get angry. When someone else gets a new car, new house, or even a new outfit or promotion we should congratulate them rather than get jealous.

One must ask, How can I love God and hate my neighbors? In the valley of jealousy, we focus on what others have instead of what God has blessed us with. Jealousy and gratitude together cannot occupy the same space. In the valley of jealousy, we should thank God for His grace and mercy and stop complaining about what we do not have.

In this valley we also will deal with the mistrust of others in our relationships and forbid them from engaging in simple conversations with others.

If and when we place our trust in God, it will
only be then that we trust others.

8

THE VALLEY OF LONELINESS

◇◇◇◇◇◇◇◇◇◇◇◇◇◇◇◇◇◇◇◇◇◇◇◇◇◇

THE VALLEY OF loneliness can be painful as well. You feel alone, isolated, and forgotten, even though you are standing in a crowd. Your valley of loneliness will make you feel disconnected from others and can have a negative effect on your well-being.

The valley of loneliness happens in our lives after we experience the loss of a close love, one such as a spouse, close friend, or even a pet.

Be encouraged in your time of loneliness. You are not alone because God has not forsaken you and He is by your side.

There is also loneliness at the top, so when you are striving for success, remember, "There is loneliness at the top."

Your loneliness may also be God-sent, for He wants this time with you, to walk with you through your valley of loneliness, to draw closer to Him, and to strengthen your faith.

The Valley of Helplessness

Many people have been in the valley of helplessness. A symptom of this valley is feeling hopeless, lifeless, or depressed. The valley of helplessness makes it hard to tackle the obstacles that you face. It is thinking that one is unable to control or change a situation because forces beyond one's control are involved. This causes one to do nothing about an issue. The **helplessness valley** leads you to think that the power to be happy and satisfied with your life is beyond your control. We all have felt this way. There will be suffering in this valley as God's people struggle with challenges and discouragement. But know that God is still present when you are in the valley of helplessness.

> *Likewise, the Spirit helps us in our weakness. For we do not know what to pray for as we ought, but the Spirit Himself intercedes for us with groanings too deep for words. And He who searches hearts knows what is the mind of the Spirit because the Spirit intercedes for the saints according to the will of God.* (Romans 8:26–27, NKJV)

Be encouraged; the Lord is by your side, and He will take you out of the valley of helplessness.

The Valley of Failure

We all experience some forms of the valley of failure, which is a common, real-life problem. No one wants to fail, and the fear of failing is unhealthy. We sometimes wish we could undo a bad decision or redo yesterday all over again and make it successful. We will often go back and forth between the valley of helplessness and the valley of failure and try to find level ground. Often this can bring disappointment and can also slow our progress as we deviate and choose another path during a dark time.

The most important thing is to learn from our mistakes and failures or we will continue on this path of failure over and over again. I know sometimes when we fail it hurts and it becomes hard to go on. Do not let your failures become your only option. Find another option to pursue; schedule some time to talk to your life's one and only advisor, God, and ask Him to guide you through your options. Don't be down on yourself because of your failure valley. Remember, we all have been through the valley of failure—some more than others—but look at them now from where you landed. I know this for sure: I've walked through the valley of failure before and I never gave up. Your failure is a part of your success in life. Talk to God about your failures and learn from them as He guides you to a more successful life.

The Valley of Disappointments

The valley of disappointment is a close friend of the valley of help-lessness—and is inevitable after the valley of failure. Most of us go through the valley of disappointment at some point in our lives. However, most of us do not look at our decision-making processes that lead us to our failures and disappointments. We often expect our journey to success as a sure thing, and we want it quick and fast.

I can recall when I got out of the military, I was preparing to go back to college. On my way home, while driving down a city bus route, I saw a former classmate standing at the bus stop, so I pulled over and asked her if she wanted a ride home. She said yes and got in the car. We talked briefly about where I had been for the last two years; I explained that I got drafted into the military. She asked, "What are your plans now?" I happily said, "I am planning on returning to Savannah State University." When I said this, she looked disapproving and she said, "You're going to school now after being gone two years?" I said yes, and she replied, "You should just get a job, because school takes too long." I just listened. I didn't want to make her feel bad, so I said, "I understand." I drove her home and dropped her off.

When I drove away I was saddened to see a young lady with a short vision of life, and I could not help her because this was her vision. I asked myself, What is four years of an investment that will affect the rest of your life? I went to college and graduated in just thirty months, and I never saw that young lady again. Your decision-making can avert the valley of disappointment.

Valley of Troubles

> *The LORD is good, a refuge in times of trouble. He cares for those who trust in him.* (Nahum 1:7, NIV)

Troubles are events waiting to happen. It is in front of you now, it lurks around the corner. It's in your pocketbook. It is in your house. It rides next to you in your car. It is in the fast-food line. It is in your relationship, job, business, your finances, family, …and yes, troubles are in the church pews sitting right next to you and shouting hallelujah and holding a Bible in their hands. The valley of troubles is on the deacon's benches and even in the church choir, singing songs about how troubles don't last always. And yes, the valley of troubles is standing in front of the pulpit preaching about troubles. The valley of trouble is in your barbershop; it is in the hair salon as you walk out after getting your hair done, looking great and feeling good until the person that greets you as you as walk out and says, "Girl, you need to have your hair done." In the valley of troubles, first "bridle your tongue." James 1:26 Secondly, that "slap response" should not be an option. How you will confront the valley of troubles is what is important. Troubles can bring us to the point of despair, anger, flight, and fight. Circumstances beyond our control can leave us depressed.

Never give up! Your drive to succeed in life and not
fail, should be driven by internal motivating factors for
self, not external motivation for pleasing others.

When you are anchored in the Lord, your troubles may be in front of you, but I am here to tell you that God will calm the troubles in your life no matter what they are.

> *Let not your heart be troubled, neither let it be afraid.* (John 14:27, NKJV)

In our troubled times in life, take your troubles to God, talk to Him, and hear His inner voice. He will lead you through your valley of troubles. God is awesome, and He hears your every cry for help, and He watches over you as you walk through your valley of troubles.

The Valley of Grief

Grief is the process of recovering from a loss. We all will experience grief due to a major loss. When we experience such a loss, we start our journey through the valley of grief. It is impossible to refuse this journey. No one loves the grief valley, but we can't shield ourselves from it. The loss of a loved one is painful and if not properly handled, can lead to an emotional breakdown. In your valley of grief, you will go through several stages.

The initial stage of grief is shock, and just like when someone goes through a physical injury, the news of the loss of a loved one will produce the same type of shock in you.

Then there is disbelief or denial of the news of the loss of a loved one. People can also feel guilty due to an unknown circumstance related to their loved ones, and then anger and then the valley of loneliness will appear in their life.

Take your time to express your emotions. Find someone to talk to. Many grieving people want to talk about their lost loved ones, but friends and family members will avoid the conversation.

Some people will even say, "I am so sorry; I know how you feel," which is a lie because unless they have lost someone just like you, there is no way that they can feel the same way you do. Going through the valley of grief is natural and inevitable in all of our lives on earth.

During my valley of grief and the loss of my dear mother, I asked myself, Where did God go? I felt so alone; I cried until I could not cry anymore. My mother was a wonderful, beautiful woman who worked almost all of her forty-six years of her life on earth, had ten children, and struggled with a heartless, abusive, lazy, alcoholic, jobless, indolent, crazy, no-good husband (and all of the other adjectives that I could think of). But you get my point. Grief is a combination of all of the good times, bad times, and pains, memories, and inner feelings after the loss of a loved one.

During my grieving periods, there was a flashback from my childhood experiences of the hard times with my mother as a child, working and trying to help her feed and clothe nine other siblings. So I became a man at nine years old, taking odd jobs to help my mother. This became my innermost feeling with the loss of my mother, plus the bitterness toward my father for his lack of being a man.

Many years later, I was able to sit down with my father to say, "Dad, I forgive you for all of the hell you put me, my mother, and my siblings through." He had no response and was silent; he just looked at me and changed the conversation. God took me through my valley of grief and I thanked Him. Be encouraged, God will take you through your valley of grief too. Remember during your grieving period, you may feel all alone, but you are never alone. God has said, "I will never leave you," so be encouraged. If you never took the time to talk to God, now is the time, for He hears your ever cry in the good times and the bad times. Talk to God right now!

The Valley of Tears

> When they walk through the Valley of Weeping, it will become a place of refreshing springs. The autumn rains will clothe it with blessings. (Psalms 84:6, NLT)

In the valley of tears, we tend to feel that our prayers are not answered by God. As disappointing as this may be, it is not His time or His will.

At some point, many of us have experienced a "weeping valley of tears" for one reason or another. This moment could have arisen from a broken heart, betrayal, or the loss of a dear friend or other loved ones. Be encouraged that God has a purpose for all of the valleys in our lives, and you will not be alone during the valley of tears. When I was thirteen years old and almost six feet tall and outgrowing all of my clothes in a family of ten children, my mother could not afford clothes for me that fit, so I suffered and wore the same outfit and worn-out tennis shoes to school every day. One morning as I was dressing for school, I looked in the mirror and realized that the one outfit I was wearing had worn out from being washed every day and it, too, did not fit anymore.

Facing reality and disappointment, I burst into tears and continued to cry until my grandmother, who was living with us, came into my room and said, "Son, why are you crying?" I said, "Grandma, I have outgrown my only outfit to wear to school."

Being a little lady in stature, she looked at my only school outfit and said, "Son, hold on; things are gonna change far ya," in her sweet Southern dialect. Her message then was encouraging to me as I was deep in the valley of tears in my life then. I got dressed for school and went to the bus stop. I missed my school bus, but a neighbor I knew was at the bus stop and said, "Marion, you missed the school bus, but the city bus is coming, and you can catch the city bus along with me." I said, "I have no bus fare." He said, "No problem," and gave me bus fare and said, "Here is some more money for you." The tears came back again, and I said, "Thanks very much."

That evening when I got home from school, my grandmother met me at the door. She said, "Son, I have something for you." She said, "The neighbor who said he gave you the bus fare this morning brought something for you." I looked at my grandmother and she had two brown paper bags in her hands. The kind neighbor had purchased me two pairs of pants with matching shirts and a new pair of tennis shoes. Of course, you know my grandmother said, "Son, I told you things will start to change for you." I looked at my grandmother as she smiled with tears of joy in her eyes. Be encouraged, the valley of tears is a place through which we all will pass; it is not where God's people dwell forever. In your valley of tears, place your trust in God, for He will take you through it.

9

THE VALLEY OF
MIRRORS

◇◇◇◇◇◇◇◇◇◇◇◇◇◇◇◇◇◇◇◇

Life is like a mirror; it's a reflection of you.

IN THE VALLEY of mirrors, there are mirrors all around you and they follow you everywhere you go. You cannot hide from or avoid the valley of mirrors because they are like your shadows and are a reflection of you. In the valley of mirrors, you cannot run away from yourself because the images you see are your reflections in the mirror and who you are.

Believe it or not, there are two of you in the mirror: your physical reflection and the reflection of you that people see of you in their world. You see, mirrors reflect an image of an object when it is hit by a light source. Without a light source, or in total darkness, we cannot see ourselves in a mirror.

These are basic rules of the laws and properties of physics and light. In our valley of mirrors, we do not see ourselves physically. This is a metaphor for what happens in the valley of mirrors and how we are seen by others. For example, people tend to see you for what they want to see and project their preconceived notions and the image of you from their perspectives.

In other words, our external world is like a giant mirror that sometimes reflects a negative and inaccurate image of us.

This can affect our lives, careers, relationships, home life, and so on. For example, during my first months at the White House as Chief Operations Officer, while walking toward a conference room in the Old Executive office building, a White House staff member approached me and asked me, "Are you a professional basketball player in the building to see the president?" I replied, "No, I work here." Being six-foot, eight-and-a-half-inches tall and a Black male, this was the image that I reflected to the White House staff person. People often perceive you to be what is reflected upon them, which is not always correct.

Some of the problems we have in our everyday life are our own reflected images being misinterpreted by others at work, in shopping centers, at home, as we drive down the streets, and even in our neighborhood and where we cross paths with others. We should emulate our teacher, God, and stop focusing on others.

> *A disciple is not above his teacher, but everyone who is perfectly trained will be like his teacher. And why do you look at the speck in your brother's eye, but do not perceive the plank in your own eye?* (Luke 6:40–41, NKJV)

What you see in the mirror is nothing but a reflection of you. That may just not be how people see you in real life because mirror images are like pieces of artwork, where interpretation may vary depending on who is looking at you, like a piece of art.

There are so many misconceived interpretations of people every day because we are human beings and we tend to see others through our own lens, which is also influenced by our upbringing, culture, and education. In the valley of mirrors, we should not judge people based on their outward reflection, their appearance.

I know of a case where a friend of mine was a new car salesman at a luxury car dealer. One day a lady walked in with hair rollers in her hair and wearing a sweatsuit. All of the salesmen in the dealership ignored her and left her standing there in the showroom because of her outer reflective appearance. No one showed an interest in helping her with a new car sale except my friend.

He walked over to the lady and asked her, "How can I help you?" The lady said, "I want to buy two BMWs, and I am prepared to write you a bank check, which you may validate through my bank."

Well, you can imagine how the rest of the story went and how the other salesmen were kicking themselves for missing this huge commission on the sale. In the valley of mirrors, there are no cheat sheets to tell you the answers in advance. Your answers will only come from the one person you were created in the image of: God. Each day when we rise and go and look in the mirror, we see ourselves, and some of us may try to form ourselves as others may want us to look, to please them. The Bible tells us that men and women are made in the image of God. It is God's image in the mirror to emulate, not man's.

> Then God said, "Let Us make man in Our image, according to Our likeness; let them have dominion over the fish of the sea, over the birds of the air, and over the cattle, over all the earth and over every creeping thing that creeps on the earth." So, God created man in His own image; in the image of God, He created him; male and female He created them. (Genesis 1:26–27, NKJV)

Most often, we look into a mirror to see how we look before going out. We will make adjustments to our hair or our clothes if we are not pleased. When we see our images being reflected wrong in a physical mirror, we obey the basic laws of physics and reflected images and make the necessary adjustments to how we look. Why is it that when we see temptation and know that it is wrong we sin anyway? This is because of our internal desires and what is in our minds as we pick and choose what is sin and not sin. Remember, there are no levels of sin. Sin is sin regardless of how it is being seen or reflected in a mirror or someone's head.

There are no smoking mirrors in life. What is in somebody's head has more to do with their personality. People see you as whatever they want you to be and are often driven by their prejudices, misjudgments, and biases. Take for example the unconscious, reflective bias from a store merchant when a person of color walks into the store or shop and the store clerk unconsciously starts to watch the store surveillance cameras. Or on the street a woman watches a person of color approaching a half block away and moves her purse closer in her grip. What is happening in these instances are preconceived notions in the minds of others. Were these actions general safety precautions? If so, why did the sight only pertain to people of color, not the others who moved among these individuals? I believe these are examples of "reflective racism." Yet most people do not want to be considered racist or capable of racist acts because they do not see themselves in the mirror.

Since their views of you are in their heads and the images are not you—not a true reflection of you—do not trouble yourself with their misconceptions and biases. Their small minds and perceptions of you do not change who you are.

The people in our personal lives are the most important ones in our mirrors. Because what is reflected back on us from them are the very qualities we want in our lives.

The valley of mirrors can be devastating because there are times in our lives when we spend too much time alone and there is little or no social reflection for us to see, which can lead to emotional problems for you. This is the time to look to God, as He is the man in the mirror in our life and He will see you as you are. He is the one who will take you through the valley of mirrors. Don't worry about what others may reflect upon you because the only harm they can do you is to break the physical mirror that reflects your image. Look in the mirror each day to face yourself. The reflected images you see are you. After all, you are the sum total of all the images being reflected from the mirror. These images include your life's experiences, your ups, and your downs. You cannot blame others for what is reflected in the mirror. So when you look in the mirror, love what you see, and live your real reflected life's images and enjoy your life.

God's mirror is a divine mirror and no man on earth can shatter His image of you, not now, tomorrow, or forever.

There was a poem that I learned at Tompkins High School in Savannah, Georgia, titled "The Man in the Glass," which explains it best.

The Man in the Glass
by Peter Dale Wimbrow, Sr.
When you get what you want in your struggle for self
And the world makes you king for a day
Just go to the mirror and look at yourself
And see what that man has to say.

For it isn't your father, or mother, or wife

Whose judgment upon you must pass

The fellow whose verdict counts most in your life

Is the one staring back from the glass.

Here's the fellow to please—never mind all the rest

For he's with you, clear to the end

And you've passed your most difficult, dangerous test

If the man in the glass is your friend.

You may fool the whole world down the pathway of years

And get pats on the back as you pass.

But your final reward will be heartache and tears

If you've cheated the man in the glass.

The Valley of Sin and Temptation

> *No temptation has overtaken you except such as is common to man.* (1 Corinthians 10:13, NKJV)

One of the oldest problems we all face is the valley of temptation and sin. Some people may want to blame Adam while others may blame Eve. No matter who you blame, it all started in the Garden of Eden and we all will pay for the original sins.

One thing is for sure: there is no classification of sins. A sin is a sin, big, little, or tiny in the eyes of God. Temptation is not sin; giving into temptation is sin. The Bible says, "but each person is tempted when they are drawn away by their own evil desires and enticed" (James 1:13–15 (NKJV).

Let no one say when he is tempted, "I am tempted by God;" for God cannot be tempted by evil, nor does He Himself tempt anyone. But each one is tempted when he is drawn away by his own desires and enticed. Then, when desire has conceived, it gives birth to sin; and sin, when it is full-grown, brings forth death.

This is simply saying our inner desires lead us into temptation, and giving in to temptations leads to sin. We all see examples of this daily in our lives where greed consumes people and they get entangled in unethical and criminal things for the sake of money. Once we take the step to act on our desires, temptation turns to sin. If you see temptation as momentary pleasure and not harmful, you will give in, but if you see it as leading to your demise and eventual incarceration for life, you will run the other direction. To avoid the valley of temptation and sin, start by taking control of your desires. Sin is like a trap, designed to keep you from the life that God has for you. So do not get caught up in a sinful trap in life.

We all have experienced the valley of temptation and sin traps. I had my experience at work at the United States Postal Service headquarters in Washington, DC. Part of my job was preparing Decisions Analysis Reports (DARs) for costly constructions of postal buildings. The report will sometimes be a couple of inches thick. I had to run copies to mail to the designated postal facility for the planning of the construction of new post offices. On occasion I would run the copies instead of asking my secretary to run the copies. The copy room was always booked and busy. Late one Friday evening before closing, I took advantage of an empty copy room and decided to run several copies of my documents.

While I was running my copies, a young lady came into the copy room and stood next to the copier where I was working. I assume she was waiting to use the copy machine. But she had nothing to copy in her hand. That didn't bother me until later, after I discovered her intention. I proceeded to copy my documents as she waited for me to finish. When I finished copying my document, I assumed she needed instructions on copying. Well, she did not. The conversation started like this. She said, "I have a favor to ask of you," and I said, "OK, I am listening."

She said, "There is a dinner at Philips Seafood tonight and I want to invite you." I asked, "What time?" She said eight o'clock, and I thought to myself, I have time to go home and pick up my wife and make it back for the free seafood! My wife, Ann, and I both love the restaurant, and besides, this will be a date night for the two of us.

But then the young lady, an industrial engineer who graduated from one of the top engineering schools, said, "Here is what I need you to do. I am picking up my mother from the National Airport at seven o'clock, and we will meet you at the restaurant. I have told my mother that I will be bringing my friend with me who is visiting from California, and she wants to meet you. And because you are supposed to be visiting from California, we must stay together to-night and Saturday night." Finally, she said, "I am OK sleeping with you for a few nights if it is OK with you."

First, I did not know how to reply. I thought perhaps I was Adam all over again and she was Eve, and instead of an apple, Eve was offering me seafood. But being a married man with a family, and a man of God, I said, "Young lady, here is the deal. First, no. Then, hell no. Secondly, I want you to face some facts." I lost the mild calm that I generally have. "I am not honored that you decided on me for your weekend lie," I said. "You're an attractive young lady and should not be pawning yourself to please your mother."

She looked at me as her eyes filled up with tears. I said, "Young lady, I am sorry, but this is not the way for you to present a man to your mother." I said, "You know I am a senior-level postal employee, and this is borderline sexual harassment." (Technically it was not, but I said this to make a point.)

"Take my advice and spend some time in church and Bible studies and perhaps you will meet a nice person to please your mother. Under no circumstance, do not lower your standards to show your mother that you have met someone." She said, "But what do I tell my mother now?"

By then, I had had enough and said, "Young lady, I do not know; make up another lie," and I walked out of the copy room.

When I got back to my office and settled down, I thought perhaps I could have handled it in a better way. But there is no better way to handle temptation and sin than the way I did—by walking away. From that day on, I never saw her in the copy room again. However, she did come by my office one day, several months later, and said that she really appreciated my advice that day, which helped her change her life. She said that she got a promotion to move to Los Angeles where she was from and would be relocating back home. I congratulated her and gave her a hug. Many months later I got an email from her that she said that she met another engineer where she was working and they were engaged to be married. In her email she also thanked me for the advice that I gave her that day in the copy room; it had changed her life. As I myself averted temptation and sin that day, I thanked God for my courage to walk away. I also gave thanks that the young lady did not ask a coworker of mine, who would have happily obliged her offer because he was a person who would sleep with a snake if asked. When we sin, it harms our relationship with God. Sin breaks that connection and stops our blessings from God.

We all have heard people say, "Don't stop my blessing." Unfortunately, we inherited sin when Adam ate the forbidden fruit, thus transmitting sin and guilt to his descendants.

I have heard people saying, "God is tempting me." No, God tempts no one! Our temptation comes at us from all directions, often when we are most vulnerable, weak, and tired. During this phase, we have no strength to fight off our temptation. Temptation can also come at us when we are at a spiritual crossroads and when we rebel against God. We all can overcome temptation by not yielding to it. Remember, "Temptation is not sin." It becomes a sin when you give into temptation. Be encouraged to stand firm. Your enemy has only limited authority; God has all authority. In the valley of temptation, always be alert and turn away from sin.

10

THE VALLEY OF HARD TIMES

◇◇◇◇◇◇◇◇◇◇◇◇◇◇◇◇◇◇◇◇◇◇◇◇

THE VALLEY OF hard times does not discriminate. It will get all of us at some point in our lives. It knocks at our door; when we refuse to let it in and walk away from the door, when we look around, it is in our house, staring us in the face. The valley of hard times is temporary and doesn't last forever, but it can be challenging when it enters your life. The valley of hard times is part of life, just as much as the good times, happy, and joyous times. The valley of hard times is just like the band of thieves and robbers hiding in the valley of shadows and death. The valley of hard times is lurking out there waiting to ambush you. When you enter the valley of a hard time, everything you see and do will give you a hard time. The truth of the matter is that no one is exempt from this. In your valley of hard times, it may appear as if everyone else is doing just fine, but this is not the case.

> *The Lord is good, a strong refuge when trouble comes. He is close to those who trust in him.* (Nahum 1:7, NLT)

God will not abandon us in our valley of hard times, and He offers us Himself as a refuge while passing through this valley. When we are in the valley of hard times, it does not mean God is punishing us. Although our wrongdoing has its own consequences, seasons of difficulty are not necessarily our fault.

> *LORD, you are my strength and fortress, my refuge in the day of trouble.* (Jeremiah 16:19, NLT)

In our life's journey, whether we are on the mountaintop or approaching a valley, we must remember our lives are about the journey that God has for us. We should not stop and give up wherever we are. Never give up. It should be at this point—in your moment of despair, as you have given it all you have—that you need to turn it over to God.

This is what God promises to do for us when we are facing hard times: He will keep you safe, He will protect you, He will be close to you, and ultimately, He will turn the situation around and pick you up when you fall down, and even carry you when you can't go on. If you stop and think about it, when there were times in your life when you were faced with impossible mountains and valleys to deal with, it was God that came through and lifted you up out of the turmoil.

Life is sometimes anything but easy. So many things have the potential to bring us to our lowest points, whether it's unfortunate life events, jobs, family, or friends, and even events in our places of worship. These events could easily make us feel unhappy in our life journey. In your valley sometimes, you can be among thousands of people and feel like the loneliest person in the world. In your valley of hard times, it is only when we fix our eyes on God that we will find the way out of the valley of hard times.

Whatever valley you are in now, remember God has not abandoned you.

His heart hurts when you hurt. He knows your struggles and your pain, and He is with you in the darkness and the light when you feel most alone.

Your prayers and cries do not fall on deaf ears, but instead, they are heard by Him, who has good plans for you and has placed you in this valley for a reason.

> *For this is why I wrote, that I might test you and know whether you are obedient in everything.* (2 Corinthians 2:9, ESV)

I know it's hard to keep believing in God when nothing seems to be going well for you and when you are deep in the valley of hard times. Everything you touch seems to fall apart, and we can't find our way out of this valley. But be encouraged, God has created this valley for you to go through to strengthen you for the dark times. Even when we can't see the goodness of God's plan, it's still there.

He has already gone before you and made your path straight for His blessing for you.

Keep going and follow His path, and every step you take leads you closer to His will and the blessing He has for you. Trust God in your journey through the valley of hard times as you will and receive His blessings. When you fall on hard times and experience difficulties, it can result in a strain on you mentally, which helps create anxiety. Our hard times can come from anywhere and anything. The most important thing to remember is that your time in the valley of hard times doesn't last forever.

11

THE VALLEY OF HATERS

*One of the worst emotional valleys in life to
journey through is the "valley of haters."*

"Haters are people who really want to be you in life."

I CAN DEFINITELY relate to this in more ways than one.
The pastor of my church that I attended a while back in Maryland
asked me to chair the church's special project, which I accepted. Being new to the area and considered to be an outsider by members of
the church and in the community, there was some resistance to me
chairing the committee. At one of the meetings, one of the members of the committee said to me, "I hate you and I cannot stand
you." I replied by saying, "I understand and I am sorry you feel this
way, and there is nothing in this world that you could do or say to
me to make me feel this way toward you." I treated her with kindness. Her entire facial expression changed when I said this. So yes,

haters are in the church. In the valley of haters, there are "jealous haters" and "evil haters."

To me a hater is no different from a jealous person. The reason is that people are jealous because of hate. Be conscious of the evil haters, for they may have the intent to cause you harm.

Haters are not on your level and definitely not your friends. They are at a level below you and see you as a threat, which is why they hate you. In the valley of haters, the haters are not your enemies because your enemies can bring you down and you know who your enemies are. Haters actually do the opposite. They validate your hierarchy in front of their peers to elevate themselves. Haters will talk about you behind your back because literally they are behind you in life and they want to be in front of you.

As you approach the valley of haters, you will see them at the entrance to the valley, eyeing you as you approach and watching every move you make. Haters will greet you as you walk into your church and haters will usher you to your seat in church. Haters are sitting right next to you every Sunday in church, and yes, haters are singing in the church choir. Haters do what is best for them: they hate. Anything you say or do will be responded to with hate or a negative response. Haters are some of the most annoying people that one can encounter. They will find a flaw in everything and anything you say or do.

In your community you will sometimes be that person or family that haters talk about. In the workplace you may become the default person when things go wrong and will get the blame from the haters on the staff.

To love God and to love one's neighbor are the greatest commandments of all. One cannot say, "I love God," but hate his/her neighbor.

> *Whoever claims to love God yet hates a brother or sister is a liar.* (1 John 4:20, NIV)

Your success in life is what creates your haters. So praise your haters for making you so successful.

> *All successful people have a long list of haters; all haters have a long list of successful people they hate.*

Haters are repeat offenders. They not only hate you, but they also hate everyone they encounter that is doing well. Haters have no joy in their lives, other than creating hate in the lives of others. Haters are the owners of the rumor mills, and they manufacture rumors about people they hate and they will sell their rumors to anyone willing to buy them. The hater is that person in a group assignment in a class or at work that shoots down everyone else's suggestions, but when asked what they would suggest, they usually have nothing.

For women the hater would see you looking great in a new dress, and rather than compliment you on how good it looks, they say, "Are you losing weight?" For men wearing a sharp new suit, the hater would say, "Oh, I have the same old suit as yours."

Haters are highly insecure and will try to put others down, which gives them pleasure. When choosing friends, be careful, because your greatest hater could be your friend. A good friend listens to and supports you and does not judge you. The hater friend will pretend to listen to your problems and will bounce your most intimate secrets to others behind your back.

The hater friend will lead you to quicksand and then throw you a straw instead of a rope and watch you sink.

The hater friend would lie to you and about you, just like a rug lying on the floor. On my way to work one morning, I once called a coworker/friend and said, "I'm on my way to my favorite coffee shop downtown." I kindly asked that coworker, "Do you want anything from the coffee shop?" The coworker said "No." So, I said, "All right, I'll see you in a few minutes." I got my coffee and headed to my office. Now when the vice president came in the office that morning and asked my coworker where I was, that same coworker lied and said, "I do not know. I have not heard from him at all this morning!"

People will hate you enough to try to get you fired.

Haters have been around for a long time and in every walk of life.

> *Everyone will hate you because of me. But not a hair of your head will perish. Stand firm, and you will win in life.* (Luke 21:17–19)

No matter how kind you are in your social interactions, there will always be someone out there who hates you. It does not matter what you do or say, how you smile; someone is going to hate you. I have seen people in my circle literally laugh when someone falls and hurts themselves, rather than come to their aid. This is a perfect kind of evil hate. To me a hater is no different from a jealous person. In the valley of haters, always be conscious of your haters because the jealous haters only want to see you fall below them, whereas the evil haters want to put you six feet below them in the ground.

Sadly, haters are hurting people and they need our prayers. So when you encounter haters, please pray and love them, that God will heal them of their hate of others.

> *But I say to you who hear: Love your enemies, do good to those who hate you, bless those who curse you, and pray for those who spitefully use you.* (Luke 6:27, NKJV)

The Valley of Mistakes

In the valley of mistakes, people often use the word *mistake* to cover up the bad decisions they made. But mistakes are something you did without conscious intentions. An example of a mistake: turning down the wrong street. But bad decisions are made intentionally.

An example: Running a red light when you know it is a violation and you could cause a serious accident and/or be fined with a point against your license and auto insurance.

We all have made mistakes in our lives, and the most important thing is that we learned from our mistakes. Most people have also made bad decisions in life and have learned from their poor judgment.

In the valley of mistakes, life's lessons don't really click in until you realize that you made a mistake or a bad decision.

First remember the difference between *mistake* and *bad decision*.

Relationship Mistakes: The person you are dating has a skull and bones tattooed on their forehead. Well, the skull and bones are labels on poisonous chemicals in your home; they are an indication of something toxic and mean "stay away." So you know this because of the tattoo, and you date this person anyway. This is a conscious intention and all of the hurt and pain will follow.

Mistakes: On the other hand, you responded to an online dating request and clicked on the wrong person and go on the date anyway.

In reality we all make mistakes, so in the valley of mistakes we should use our mistakes to learn from as our trials and tribulations. In the valley of mistakes, as we grow closer to God, we will make fewer mistakes. Mistakes are for learning, not repeating the same thing over and over again.

> *The steps of a good man are ordered by the Lord, And He delights in his way. Though he falls, he shall not be utterly cast down; For the Lord upholds him with His hand.* (Psalms 37:23–24, NKJV)

In the valley of mistakes, use your mistakes to make you stronger in your faith and not foolish. If you dwell on your past mistakes, it will only cause you to make them again and again, so move on.

The Valley of Regrets

In the valley of regrets, we want to be repentant of something that has happened or we regret a missed opportunity. One can reasonably say that regrets usually follow our times in the valley of mistakes. We sometimes need to look backward to move forward, but don't waste your time regretting the way things were and wishing you could go back to yesterday. Remember that God is sovereign, powerful, and will be there with you every step of the way. That regrettable event in your past was just a training assignment to prepare you for the road ahead.

We all have had moments when we experienced things we have done and things we said, things that we all want to take back. You must remember that the words that come out of your mouth are like toothpaste coming out of a tube: you cannot put them back.

When we think back, many people would say that temptation and sins are some of the many regrets that we all have in life. But remember, Jesus has washed us of all our sins. He paid for our earthly failures and sins on the cross.

So be encouraged and cast aside your regrets and start looking forward and not backward. In the midst of temptation and sin, thank God that He saved you and has forgiven you of all of your sins.

No More Regrets
I wish I had more time.
I would watch more sunrises.
I wish I had more time.
I would laugh more and cry less.
I wish I had more time.
I would spend less time at work.
I wish I had more time.
I would dance every night.
I wish I had more time.
I would play in the snow.
I wish I had more time.
I will hug all the children more.
I wish I had more time.
I will hug and kiss my wife every day.
I wish I had more time.
I would hug my nine siblings.
I wish I had more time.
I would make the world a better place.

I wish I had more time.

I would read the Bible every day.

I wish I had more time.

I would have no more regrets.

Have no more regrets.

Live your life every day and be blessed.

You see, to live life without regrets does not mean that you will never wish you had done something different or not made mistakes or failed. What it does mean, is that you will live your life every day to the fullest.

We all must spend and live our lives with self-awareness and love of God. When given an opportunity, no matter what it is, give it all you've got. Whatever happens will happen, and you will have no more regrets.

The Valley of Pride

Pride can be defined as a feeling of deep pleasure or satisfaction in an achievement or an accomplishment. It also can be described as egotism concerning one's own appearance or status and not just something that's been accomplished. In the valley of pride, we often have an inflated sense of our own worth or personal status, and typically this makes us feel a sense of superiority over others. We can easily put others down to further lift ourselves up.

Today pride is not just a problem for individuals; it is a problem for humanity. I believe, from what I've read in the Bible, that pride is at the root of all sin.

In our valley of pride, we will misplace our sense of worth: "In his pride the wicked man does not seek him; in all his thoughts there is no room for God." (Psalm 10:4) Pride is the opposite of humility; this is what we read in Proverbs 11:2: "When pride comes, then comes disgrace, but with humility comes wisdom." This is why "patience is better than pride." (Eccl 7:8) The problem with pride is that we have placed ourselves on a pedestal which makes it difficult for others to communicate with us because we feel above everyone. We should humble ourselves—or God will do it for us.

Pride is sin and is considered a rebellion against God because of the focus on our attributes of self and not on God. In reality there is nothing wrong with praising one's self, but when it becomes excessive and self-focus is exclusive, it becomes a sin. In the valley of pride, pride is a sin because it presumes that we are perfect, which we are not. All the glory belongs to God. With our pride we constantly critique others. This is very prevalent in our churches and community. We tend to judge others on their spiritual conditions based on their outward appearances.

> *God opposes the proud. But gives grace to the humble.* (1 Peter 5:5, NET)

As Jesus said, "Those who exalt themselves will be humbled, and those who humble themselves will be exalted." (Matt 23:12) In your valley of pride, do not let your pride get in the way of an eternal life.

The Valley of Guilt

Your valley of guilt is the result of having violated a specific rule or law. We all have experienced guilt one way or another in our lives. When we cross a moral, ethical, or legal line, we are guilty. This is true even if we did not know a line was crossed. I believe guilt is primarily a state or condition, not a feeling. According to the Bible, we are all guilty before God. (Romans 3:10, 23) The fact that a person may not "feel guilty" does not affect his or her guilty status legally or morally. Our guilt started when Adam and Eve broke God's law against eating the forbidden fruit. As I have stated, some may blame Eve, others may blame Adam, but regardless of who you blame, they still violated God's law. They knew they had violated a specific law. They were guilty and they felt guilty. God demonstrated His plan to cover human guilt with the shedding of innocent blood. (Genesis 3:21) Our world today is filled with condemnation and hopelessness. In the valley of guilt, we need first to pray and ask God to reveal any sins for which we may be under conviction. If God reveals such a sin, let the believer follow the three steps God outlines for our restoration: confess, repent, and, if necessary, make restitution. In the valley of guilt, if you feel guilty for something you said or did to someone, say, I am sorry, right away, and make your apology unconditional. We have been justified. (Romans 5:1) God has placed all our sin on His own Son. (2 Corinthians 5:21) He has taken the righteousness of Christ and granted it to us.

That divine exchange guarantees our acceptance by God and eternal life with Him. (2 Corinthians 5:18–19; Romans 5:9–10) When we fail we have God's promise that, if we confess our sins to Him, He will forgive us and wipe away all traces of guilt. (1 John 1:9)

The Valley of Pain and Hurt

The valley of pain and hurt will be one of the most challenging journeys of our lives. I can honestly confess that this was and still is one of my most challenging valleys. My heart and soul have cried out many times in this valley, but God took my hand and He led me through. You see, God will purposefully lead you through the valleys to the other side of the mountain. It is not a matter of *if* we will pass through a trial, obstacle, or period of pain and hurt, it is a matter of *when*. In the valley of pain and hurt, you will not only experience physical pain, but emotional and mental pain. At some point in our lives, we all will experience some form of physical pain, which could come from anything because we are human. We can seek medical help to get us through our physical pain. But then we come to our mental and emotional pain and hurt. This is the deep pain that hurts us inside. This could be from the troubles in our everyday lives. This is also when we will need the external support and care of our mental health care specialist to help us through this valley, as well as prayers and our faith.

> *Now faith is confidence in what we hope for and assurance about what we do not see.* (Hebrews 11:1, NIV)

My faith has been my anchor and continues to keep me grounded during times in the valley of pain and hurt. In the valley of pain and hurt, God knows the way, and He will lead you to the other side of the mountain. In your valley of pain and hurt, know that God is on your side, despite your desperation, desire, and intention to give up in life. God loves us so much that sometimes He will send someone that He can trust to intervene, to change our trajectory when we least expect it.

I know this for sure because I had to intervene in a person's life before. On one Sunday my wife Ann and I were heading home after church, and we decided to pick up a carry-out food order to enjoy a quiet Sunday afternoon together. On our way home from the restaurant where we picked up the food, it appeared that every red light was stuck on red. We wanted to get home before our food got cold.

At the very last red light, just before I was about to make the turn for home, I looked ahead and I could see an image on a rail on the overpass bridge overlooking the fast-moving interstate highway traffic.

When the red light changed, and as I began my approach to the bridge, I saw a man sitting on the rail, about to jump. I stopped my car, put on my emergency flashers, got out and ran toward the man. The man on the bridge said, "Stop. I want to die today." I said, "Let me pray for you." He said, "No, I am in pain and I want to die." I used my conversation with him to inch closer to him. When I was at arm's length. I said, "OK, since you want to die today, let me pray with you before you jump." He turned around to look at me in shock and then turned around to jump. I grabbed him and pulled him to safety. But I learned one thing from this event. When a person wants to commit suicide, do not let them outsmart you. He then said to me, "I'm OK," and I let him go. He then ran around my car and back toward the rail to jump. He was very fast and outran me. When I got within arms' reach of him, I tackled him and held him down until another motorist came to help me hold him. Ann, my wife, called the police and an ambulance. You see, God is on our side. We should not let our everyday problems and the valley of pain and hurt get us down, no matter what.

The Valley of Liars

A faithful witness does not lie, but a false witness breath out lies. (Proverbs 14:4)

In the valley of liars, there is a side to God which cannot be ignored, regarding His view on those who speak lies. Some people live their lives lying to their family and friends. It's been said "everyone lies" or "it's OK to lie once in a while." If this is the case, how can you trust anyone, including your spouse, family members, friends, your medical doctor, your parents, or anyone? The ones who say everyone lies clearly reveal their own defective character. No, not everyone lies. There are people who live their lives honorably and with integrity. One of the seven deadly sins God hates is a lying tongue. (Proverbs 6:16–17) A person who lies hates the individual they are lying to. (Proverbs 26:28)

God hates the sin of lying because it is deceptive. False prophets and teachers are equally condemned. Both are compared to irrational wild animals with destructive behavior. Such liars have no respect for others. They don't care who they hurt or destroy. God hates the act of lying because it goes contrary to His truth. Truth is what God offers to man. To follow His truth is to reject the ideology everyone lies. If you are living by the word of God, then you, too, should reject the notion that lying is OK. But in our world today, lying has become the new normal. Every day we see and hear lies upon lies from everyone from our elected officials, people we know and trust, and even those standing in front of the pulpits in our places of worship.

People who lie learn very quickly how they can manipulate other people.

The fact remains that many people lie to get other people to do what they want them to do. People who lie to manipulate a situation or other people are often only interested in personal gain and don't care about other people and the consequences of their lies.

However, it is important to note that a liar manipulates a situation and a person's thoughts, even a lie that is told with innocent intentions. What we say and do has an effect on others and even well-intended lies are a form of manipulation.

In the valley of lying, we get trapped in an uncomfortable situation because we expect others to treat us honorably and tell the truth. We expect not to be lied to. When the lie is told, we lose faith and trust in the other person. There are some people who lie frequently and do not care about the effects of their lies. These people lie so much even they can believe their own lies. Take, for an example, a political candidate who lies to win an election He will soon keep lying, even after winning the election, and should not be trusted. This type of person also typically does not care about others' opinions about their lies. Most people, however, care how others treat them, and knowing they were lied to can be a breach of trust, depending on the gravity of the lie. In the valley of liars, you must avoid the liars, to protect yourself from the consequences of their lies.

> *Deliver me, O Lord, from lying lips, from deceitful tongue.*
> (Psalm 120:2)

12

THE VALLEY OF SPIRITUAL DARKNESS

THE VALLEY OF spiritual darkness is not a place of physical darkness, but the state of a person who is living apart from God in darkness.

Today as we all look around our country and the world, we see evidence of people living in spiritual darkness. Many have forsaken God for the comforts of evil in the valley of spiritual darkness. The darkness in this valley represents the separation of man from God and being overcome by the evils of the world. Just like sin separates us from one another, it also separates us from God. We are lying if we say we have a fellowship with God but continue to lie and live in spiritual darkness by continuing to perpetuate the lies. Every day many of us see people living in spiritual darkness as they pretend to have a fellowship with God through Jesus Christ, but then they commit some horrible things and inflict pain and hurt upon others.

It is because of clouds of spiritual darkness that these horrific events are happening in the world and our country today. We have turned away from God's love and have accepted the comforts of the spiritual darkness and evils that lurk there. The valley of spiritual darkness exists on every street and in our everyday walks of life. So remember, our spiritual darkness means not having a fellowship with God through a relationship with Jesus Christ.

One of the most important reasons for the spiritual darkness of society today is due to the decline of our religious institutions and the belief in God. The external manifestation of evil, hate, greed, and power is growing at an alarming rate. Many of our great religious institutions have great preachers, ministers, but not shepherds of God. The weakening of the core foundations of our religious institutions has helped broaden the valley's evils and spiritual darkness. Our valley experiences in our lives are temporary, but many people find comfort in the valley of spiritual darkness and tend to dwell there in comfort. They have found comfort and a relationship with the forces of evil instead of God. We all must ask ourselves, Have they found comfort or is it just evil? Some of the greatest traps in the valley of spiritual darkness are "the tricks of the devil." You see, the devil is the master of deception. He will try to deceive you by convincing you that he does not exist. So then, you enter the valley of spiritual darkness, where the devil surrounds you with his followers of evil, hate, sin, and temptation, greed, and power. This is a place where evils and ungodliness run rampant. If you do not believe this, just take a look around; it is actually happening in our world today right before your eyes. You can see the erosion of honesty and integrity, with lies upon lies, the emerging of hate groups using social media as their platforms, the growing political and election turmoil, voter intimidation, political corruptions, killing on our city streets across America, and mass shooting after mass shooting by those who hate.

But there is hope, and those who walk with God will find the valley of spiritual darkness uninviting and reject the darkness for the lights of God. You see, God is the one and only light that keeps shining even in the places of darkness, and nothing can extinguish the light of God. Some may have the ability to see the light of God, but decline to accept it, and will find comforts with the evil forces in the valley of spiritual darkness and will perish there. This is because the unbelievers live in the valley of spiritual darkness, which has blinded their minds and vision so that they do not want to see the lights of God. This is evident in our world because some see and hear the lies upon lies and turn a blind eye to truth and integrity for the comforts of evils. The valley of spiritual darkness is sometimes revealed in ordinary language and everyday occurrences and right in front of you. Your greatest adversaries are not people you don't know of, but the spiritual wickedness and evils in high places are using their political platforms to increase their followers of evil, power, greed, divisiveness, and hate. In the valley of spiritual darkness, it is the desire of the devil to bring you under his total control.

On Earth when the sun goes down, darkness falls upon the earth and upon all of God's creatures, but there will always be light for true believers of God. Be encouraged, just as the sun goes down, it will rise again on another day. But for some people, the sun will never shine upon them because of their preference of spiritual darkness and the evil, power, greed, and hate that come with it.

There has been increasing spiritual darkness in America for quite some time. The fallacy of this is that within our great country, we have individuals willing to take advantage of a broken system. And the most troubling thing about this is these individuals will take advantage of a broken system rather than try to fix it.

This is the evil of spiritual darkness; it can be seen across America with the coming of new hate groups and newly elected public officials.

The valley of spiritual darkness is in opposition to the light of God's love in Christ.

If Christ walked on Earth and opened the eyes of the blind, He surely can bring man out of the valley of spiritual darkness through His love. No matter how deep the darkness is in the valley of spiritual darkness, the light of God will overcome all evils that separates us from Him.

The Valley of Spiritual Warfare

In our world and country today, we all must fight against the forces of evil and spiritual darkness. I believe we must pray and pray and use all of our spiritual powers to fight against this spiritual darkness:

> Finally, my brethren, be strong in the Lord and in the power of His might. Put on the whole armor of God, that you may be able to stand against the wiles of the devil. For we do not wrestle against flesh and blood, but against principalities, against powers, against the rulers of the darkness of this age, against spiritual hosts of wickedness in the heavenly places. Therefore, take up the whole armor of God, that you may be able to withstand in the evil day, and having done all, to stand. Stand therefore, having girded your waist with truth, having put on the breastplate of righteousness, and having shod your feet with the preparation of the gospel of peace; above all, taking the shield of faith with which you will be able to quench all the fiery darts of the wicked one. And take the helmet of salvation, and the sword of the Spirit, which is the word of God; praying always with all prayer and supplication in the Spirit, being watchful to this end with all perseverance and supplication for all the saints.
> (Ephesians 6:10–18, NKJV)

My life experiences have taught me all about battles and wars, being a Vietnam veteran. I learned that battles are fought on different

MARION DEVOE SR.

fronts, for different reasons, and with varying degrees of intensity.
It's not all jungle warfare or urban warfare. The same is true in our
valley of spiritual warfare against the forces of evils. Our spiritual
warfare began when God declared war on Satan.

> *And I will put enmity between you and the woman, and between
> your seed and her Seed; He shall bruise your head, and you shall
> bruise His heel.* (Genesis 3:15, NKJV)

In our spiritual warfare, we are faced with three enemies: the
world, our flesh, and the devil. (Ephesians. 2:1–3) In our nation
today, some of our elected officials are part of the evil forces and
authorities that we all must battle against in our spiritual warfare.

We are in a spiritual warfare for our souls and our nation. The
enemy seeks total control over all of us by encouraging dissent between us and preventing us from uniting on a common battlefront
with lies upon lies and deception. This is one of the oldest battle
strategies: divide and conquer. Many of us can see this being done
across our nation. In our world today, the evil forces are all around
us and have us under siege and have impacted our lives on a daily
basis and on all fronts, and many are struggling while others are not
aware.

Our struggles are not only just our economics, but with the forces of evil.

And you He made alive, who were dead in trespasses and sins, in which you once walked according to the course of this world, according to the prince of the power of the air, the spirit who now works in the sons of disobedience, among whom also we all once conducted ourselves in the lusts of our flesh, fulfilling the desires of the flesh and of the mind, and were by nature children of wrath, just as the others. (Ephesians 2:1–3, NKJV)

This is a spiritual war, ongoing for the hearts and souls of man as the forces of evil seek to turn us away from God. Be mindful that evil forces can only enter your heart if you allow it. I have heard many people say, "The devil made me do it." Well, I am here to tell you that, yes, the devil tempts us, but we choose to sin.

The devil is the master of disguise, deception, and distraction, and a liar, who entices us to follow him with false promises and lies. He does this by keeping us apart from one another, by dividing us. In several of the chapters in this book, I mentioned the valleys in our lives. Well, these valleys are where Satan hangs out and would like to keep us there by deceiving, distracting, and discouraging us.

But I have also mentioned that God will walk with you through the darkest time in your life, and He will provide the light for each one of us when we are in our valleys of darkness and free us from the evil forces of the darkness.

> *Your word is a lamp to my feet and a light to my path.* Psalms 119:105, NKJV)

What is important is that we must remember that evil forces are everywhere, in our political system, our communities, workplaces, and even in our places of worship. Many of us do not and cannot see them or do not believe that we have evil spiritual forces attacking us.

These attitudes, beliefs, and convictions will not help us to win this battle. I am by no means a biblical scholar, but I know that Jesus came and conquered and won this battle and the war is already won in the heavenly realm: "All authority has been given to Me in heaven and on earth." (Matthew 28:18) We now have the privilege of having an eternal relationship with God. Yes, through the resurrection power of Jesus and the Holy Spirit.

Our everyday victory is achieved by knowing, believing, and understanding the battles that we are enduring daily have already been won. All we need to do to shield off the evil forces of our enemies on all spiritual battlefronts is to use the most powerful shield of armor in the world, which is God's word/scripture. His words will sustain us and bring us victory on all spiritual battlefronts.

The more we receive God's spirit, the less we will be threatened by the forces of spiritual darkness.

THE OTHER SIDE OF THE MOUNTAIN

Coming Out of Life's Valleys

God desires that we continually to live on the mountaintop of His victory for us. It is true that we will go through valleys in our lives as we journey through life, fighting a spiritual warfare. What we must remember is that God is in control, whether we are on the mountaintop or in the valleys. Every one of us will go through valley experiences. God allows us to go through the valleys to prepare us for our life's journeys. You see, our valleys are a training ground for our spiritual warfare. No soldier became a great warrior without some serious training. But just like getting to be a great warrior, there will be tough battles in our spiritual warfare.

> *You therefore must endure hardship as a good soldier of Jesus Christ. No one engaged in warfare entangles himself with the affairs of this life, that he may please him who enlisted him as a soldier.* (2 Timothy 2:3–4, NKJV)

We must always keep in mind that God's grace and His mercy will never fail us, no matter what battles we face on Earth.

The Other Side of the Mountain

Mountains, of course, are a natural elevation of the earth's surface, but they also represent metaphorically seemingly insurmountable obstacles in life. We all have mountains, but we also have God to get us over them. I defined valleys as an elongated depression between uplands, hills, or mountains. In reality our life's journey takes us to the mountaintop: a place of revelation and inspiration. Your mountaintop experience does not mean that your problems and worries are all over. The mountaintop experience is where we meet God. We all love being on the mountaintop, a place where we can feel God's presence, where we can clearly hear God's voice. I can recall going to the top of a mountain in Colorado Springs, and at the top there was no noise. The silence was like being in the vacuum of space. It is a place like this where we all can focus on God while towering above all of the worldly things. Our mountaintop experience will paint a clear picture of God's divine plans for all of us. But it is inevitable that we will journey down the mountain into the valleys, where we meet our challenges and struggles. We all will experience both the mountaintop and the valleys in life. This is because life is filled with ups and downs, and most of us will spend a lot of time in the valleys. Think about the valley that you are in today.

The valley is very different than the mountaintop; the valley is where life becomes challenging; the valley is where many battles are fought and where feelings are hurt and our tears flow freely. Valleys are where our attitudes are developed and changed. The valley is the place where we meet our fears, our dreams are shattered, we experience failures, grief, haters, loneliness, betrayal, pain and disappointments, and guilt. Be encouraged! Our valleys are temporary. God has a reason for each valley experience for everyone, be it spiritual warfare or because of our own rebellious actions. Remember, our mountaintop is where we go to meet God, but the valley is where God comes to us.

You see, God will take you through your valleys, no matter what type of valley you are in now, even while reading this book. So it is OK to cry out now and let your tears flow freely because God will take you through your valley that you are in now.

God watches over us. He does not watch over us from outside of the valleys; He does not watch over us from the mountaintops because He is with us as we walk through the valleys in our life. When you are deep in the valleys of life, there is only one way out of your valley and that is through God's will and mercy, and with prayers.

Our lives can change overnight and that mountaintop can come crumbling down, and we will find ourselves deep in the valleys of our lives, feeling all alone and in despair. You see, when we are on a mountaintop in life, we praise God. But how can we praise Him on the mountaintop and then feel all alone in the valleys?

We must then ask ourselves, Where is our faith? When we are on a mountain, we can see things clearly from above, and we will not be able to see and feel the problems in the valleys. But in valleys we will find ourselves in the thick of things and not above it all. This is when we need to pray and ask God to take control and walk with us. Our valley experiences are difficult times in our lives, and we all must learn how to navigate through them.

We're living in a world today on steroids, where everything is accelerated, which makes our valley experiences even more challenging. Modern-day technology has elevated our everyday personal life. Lying has become the new normal. Many of us are facing life's problems as we move through a rapidly paced life, and things are starting to unravel right before our eyes. We all must stop to remember that our main problem is that we have left God out of the picture. Remember, no matter how perfect we are, our life's problems aren't going anywhere unless we begin to face them head-on and take our problems to God. In our lives today, we often become too self-centered rather than relying on God to gain a meaningful life. Our everyday life will bring us tears, pain, financial problems, grief, fears, hardship, and betrayal: watch out for those who cause divisiveness and place obstacles in your way because they are not serving God.

Lastly, we all have a purpose here in this life and we all will eventually fulfill our purpose in life. Some of us will take a little longer than others to find our real purpose. We should pray to God, and He will reveal it to us along the way. I have seen many people in my life who found their purpose and carried it out.

One such case is my wife's relative, who found her purpose long ago and carried it out until she was approaching her ninetieth birthday. God bless her, Mrs. Eloise Johnson, my wife's aunt, a prayer warrior in the community. She wore several hats and helped everyone in the community; she was a great cook, a mechanic, a carpenter, a medic, a plumber, a coach, a lifeguard, an electrician…she provided a host of community services. You see, she knew her purpose in life and she asked God for guidance and carried it out.

Even as she was approaching her late eighties, she worked on a food drive for the community to feed the hungry by delivering food to the needy across the community in Garden City, Georgia.

As she grew older, her driving ability was a little troublesome, so the authorities eventually took her driver's license away. So Mrs. Johnson took her riding lawnmower—that she used to cut neighbors' lawns for free—to drive around the community and delivered food to the needy.

Then the community police authority told her that she could not use the lawnmower on city streets to deliver the food. She then found a little red wagon to pull over the roads to deliver the food.

Finally, the authorities stopped her from using the city streets to pull the wagon along to deliver food. Mrs. Johnson asked God to give her strength, and in her late eighties, she then walked for miles carrying food to the needy.

You see, in each of the problems that Mrs. Johnson encountered along the way, she prayed about it first and asked God to guide her along the way, to give her strength, and to protect her as she journeyed through life to the other side of the mountain.

Psalm 23: A Psalm of David

The LORD is my shepherd;
I have all that I need.
He lets me rest in green meadows;
he leads me beside peaceful streams.
He renews my strength.
He guides me along the right paths,
bringing honor to his name.
Even when I walk
through the darkest valley,
I will not be afraid,
for you are close beside me.
Your rod and your staff
protect and comfort me.
You prepare a feast for me
in the presence of my enemies.
You honor me by anointing my head with oil.
My cup overflows with blessings.
Surely your goodness and unfailing love will pursue me
all the days of my life,
and I will live in the house of the LORD
forever. Amen.

Prayer: God, help us to learn from our mountain experiences. God, walk with us through our valleys and protect us. God, help us to learn as an act of repentance. Amen.

Our lives are a series of mountains and valleys, and each one serves a purpose, even though they are metaphoric in a sense. But to us they appear to be real. The mountains and valleys are challenging in our lives. They are tough to negotiate and we suffer through the storms. In our life's journeys, we will experience fear and anxiety and sometimes our tears will flow freely. The reason why we struggle in our journeys is that we leave God out of our plans. Remember, God created the earth and mountains and valleys, so surely He can guide and protect you through your metaphoric mountains and valleys. He places us on our journeys in life to prepare us to receive His blessings. Remember the phrase, "Faith moves mountains."

> *Truly I tell you, if you have faith as small as a mustard seed, you can say to this mountain, "Move from here to there," and it will move; and nothing will be impossible for you.* (Matthew 17:20, NKJV)

So what do you have faith in? Our faith is in God. As I have stated, God created the mountains and the valleys and, surely, He can move them in your life. My favorite Bible scripture regarding faith was Peter walking on the water. We must first look at the setting in which this took place. (Matthew 14:28–29, NKJV)

Following the occasion of the feeding of the five thousand, Jesus instructed His disciples to board a ship and cross the Sea of Galilee while He remained behind to send away the multitude and to pray.

A windstorm arose on the sea during the voyage, and the small ship was tossed among the waves. To add to their distress, the disciples were confronted with what they thought was a spirit, and they cried out in fear. What they saw was Jesus walking on the water. Although the Savior announced that it was He, whom they need not fear, some on the ship were skeptical. Peter challenged, "If it is thou, bid me come unto thee on the water." And Jesus responded, "Come."

Peter left the boat and, like Jesus, walked on the water. But when Peter's attention was diverted from Jesus to the buffeting winds around him, his faith began to weaken, and he began to sink helplessly into the water. He cried out, appealing to Jesus for help. After clasping Peter's hand and assuring his safety, Jesus mildly chastised Peter: "O you of little faith, why did you doubt?" This is a powerful example of believing in God and having faith. So as you climb your mountains in life and walk through your valleys, have faith in God, for he will deliver you.

My advice and prayers for you are to slow down and let go of your problems, have faith, and let God guide your life as you journey up the mountain and through the valleys to the other side of the mountain: a place where God will bless you tremendously.

Amen.

The Other Side of the Mountain

On the other side of the mountain, we will have joy,

and love, because God is our Shepherd.

On the other side of the mountain, my trials will be behind me,

And my future will be in front of me.

On the other side of the mountain, my enemies are before me,

and I know who they are.

On the other side of the mountain, even when

I walk through the darkest valley,

I will not be afraid,

for I know God is my Shepherd.

On the other side of the mountain, there will

be no more tears of hurt or pain,

only tears of joy.

On the other side of the mountain, I will

walk away from temptation,

walk toward God, and be blessed.

On the other side of the mountain, hat-

ers will see themselves in the mirror,

and their reflections will bear the truth about them.

On the other side of the mountain, I will

look forward and not backward

and have no more regrets.

On the other side of the mountain, I will lower my pride

and have no guilt, pain, or hurt.

On the other side of the mountain, my cup will overflow
with His blessings and His goodness,
and unfailing love will follow me all the days of my life.
On the other side of the mountain is where I will have faith,
live my life for God, and receive His blessing forever and ever.
Amen.

Psalm 121 (NLT)
A song for pilgrims ascending to Jerusalem

I look up to the mountains,
does my help come from there?
My help comes from the LORD,
who made heaven and earth!
He will not let you stumble,
the one who watches over you will not slumber.
Indeed, he who watches over Israel,
never slumbers or sleeps.
The LORD himself watches over you!
The LORD stands beside you as your protective shade.
The sun will not harm you by day,
nor the moon at night.
The LORD keeps you from all harm,
and watches over your life.

MARION DEVOE SR.

> The LORD keeps watching over you as you come
> and go, both now and forever. Amen.

In your life's journey, I encourage you to incorporate into your daily prayers some of the scriptures at the end of some of the passages in this book as they may apply to you along your life's journey. The words of God will help you climb the mountains and walk through valleys in your life.

ACKNOWLEDGMENTS

I would like to acknowledge my wife, Ann Devoe, for her contributions to this book and Sylvia Taylor for her spiritual support. The late coach Jerome Jinks, my high school basketball coach at Tompkins High School in Savannah, Georgia, encouraged me to be all that I can be in life.

INDEX

A

Accountable

When spiritual leaders in African American or White churches are not held accountable for their actions
Page 15

African American churches

The African American churches throughout most of America's history were the pillars of faith and hope and encouragement for the communities of people of color.
Page 12, 15

All successful people

All successful people have a long list of haters; all haters have a long list of successful people they hate
Page 117

Armor of God

Therefore, take up the whole armor of God, that you may be able to withstand in the evil day, and having done all, to stand.
Page 135,138

Autocratic leadership

It is my opinion that true shepherds of God are selfless leaders, whereas the bullying autocratic church leaders are selfish, only interested in themselves at the expense of others.
Page 14

Authority is given to me

"All authority has been given to Me in heaven and on earth." We now have the privilege of having an eternal relationship with God." Matthew 28:18
Page 138

B

Back on your feet

"When God places you back on your feet, after a broken relationship, stay away from those who knocked you down."
Page 31

Betrayal

"People will betray you for thirty pieces of silver as they did Jesus." Matthew 26:15
Page 86

Black dress lady

The young lady had on a black dress with designs of leaves that matched the surrounding burnt, bright orange leaves falling from the trees lining Seventeenth Street.
Page 5

C

Churches

"Churches are a place where evil should flee, but have become a refuge for evil.
Page 16

Church hierarchy,
Individualism, self-branding, showmanship, money, power, greed, and external political interest, events not related to churches and the Bible
Page 14

Cicada bugs
The cicadas are about one-and-a-half inches long with red beady eyes; they fly, poorly, into everything and everybody. They were like locusts flying and destroying crops. Meanwhile, I did not
Page 6

Civil War never ended
Often, I hear mainstream media talks about the United States being on the verge of another civil war. When I think back to my high school history classes, the truth is, the original United States Civil War never ended
Page 11

Climbing earthly mountains
"When climbing your earthly mountain in life, your goal is to avoid the evils of man by bridging a path/route around the evils and continue your climb up your mountain."
Page 25

Creation of man: Man, creation was not an experiment
"God did not create you in his image as an experiment," Genesis1:27
Page 41

D

Divisiveness throughout America
>With their racist conspiracy theories and lies upon lies in hopes of influencing our political, social, and economic systems of governing
>Page 24

Divine mirror
>God's mirror is a divine mirror and no man on earth can shatter His image of you, not now, tomorrow, or forever.
>Page 104

E

Evil haters,
>For they may have the intent to cause you harm.
>Haters are not on your level and definitely not your friends
>Page 116

F

Faith
>With which you will be able to quench all the fiery darts of the wicked one
>Page 135

Faith moves mountains
>"Truly I tell you, if you have faith as small as a mustard seed, you can say to this mountain" Matthew 17:20
>Page 145

Faith: Peter walking on water
"O thou of little faith, wherefore did thou doubt?" Matt. 14:28–
Page 146

Faith
"Now faith is confidence in what we hope for and assurance
Page 127

Fear
"For God hath not given us the spirit of fear, but of power, and
love, and a sound mind."
2 Timothy 1:7
Page 56

Fear not
"Fear not, for I am with you." Isaiah 41:10
Page 54

Fool's love
"Never fall for fool's love, because fool's love is like fool's gold,
which is nothing but a worthless piece of stone."
Page 34

G

God is our refuge
"God is our refuge when trouble comes. He is close to those who
trust in Him." Nahum 1:7
Page 92

God is the mirror to emulate
"God is the mirror to emulate, not man."
Page 102

God, you are my strength and fortress
"God, you are my strength and fortress, my refuge in the day of trouble." Jeremiah 16:19.
Page 117

H

Happy, Making her/him happy
"If you make her/him happy, she/he will make you happy. If you make her/him unhappy, she/he will make you unhappy."
Page 39

Hate: Everyone will hate you
"Everyone will hate you because of me. But not a hair of your head will perish. Stand firm, and you will win in life." Luke 21:17–19
Page 118

Haters: The hater friend and quicksand
"The hater friend will lead you to quicksand and then throw you a straw, instead of a rope and watch you sink."
Page 118

I

If a man says, I love God
"If a man says, I love God and hate his brother, he is a liar." 1 John 4:20
Page 117

K

King, Treat him like a king
If you treat him like a king, he will become your king."
Page 42

L

Lie down at night: Proverbs 3:24
"When you lie down at night, you will not be afraid, your sleep will be sweet."
Page 55

"Love should not hurt, 1
Love is not jealous, love is not hate, love
is not anger, love is not mean."
Page .39

M

Man in the glass
When you get what you want in your struggle for self
And the world makes you king for a day
Just go to the mirror and look at yourself
And see what that man has to say.
Page 104

Men and women
Build monuments and structures with their
hands and then destroy them with their mouths."
Page 3

Mirrors,
Emulate your teacher, stop focusing on others." Luke 6:34–41
Page 102

O

Obedience
"For this is why I wrote, that I might test you and know whether you are obedient in everything." 2 Corinthians 2:9
Page 113

Original Sin
"One of the oldest problems we all face in life is the valley of temptation and sin. Some people may want to blame Adam, while others may blame Eve. No matter whom you blame it all started in the Garden of Eden and we all will pay for the original sins." Genesis 3–6
Page 105

Other Side of the mountain poem
The Other Side of the Mountain
On the other side of the mountain, we will have joy,
and love, because God is our Shepherd.
Page 148

P

Piccolo
There was a man on the truck nicknamed "Piccolo" who I would often see in my community standing on the street corners playing the harmonica
Page 20

Psalm of David
The Lord is my shepherd;
I have all that I need.
He lets me rest in green meadows;
Page 144

Psalm 23: A Psalm of David
"Even when I walk through the darkest valley, I will not be afraid for you are close beside me." Psalm 23:4
Page 72

Psalm 121
A song for pilgrims ascending to Jerusalem
I look up to the mountains,
does my help come from there?
My help comes from the Lord,
Page 149

Prayer
Prayer: God, help us to learn from our mountain experiences. God, walk with us through our valleys and protect us. God, help us to learn as an act of repentance. Amen. Page 145

Q

Queens,
Men: "Remember, if you treat her like a queen, you will become her king. " Women:
Page 42

R

Race-Inflicted Stress
Stress can be inflicted upon you in more than one way. I believe that race-inflicted stresses are mountains. The results of America's hate groups, political extremism, and White Nationalism culminate in America's systemic racism.
Page 8

Regrets poem
I wish I had more time. I would watch more sunrises.
I wish I had more time.
I would laugh more and cry less.
I wish I had more time.
Page 122

Retribution Theology
"Retribution theology is the belief that those who are obedient to God are called righteous and will be blessed, while those that are disobedient are wicked and will be cursed" (2006).
Page 1

Revenge, I will` take
Dear friends, never take revenge. Leave that to the righteous anger of God. For the Scriptures say, "I will take revenge; I will pay them back," says the Lord. (Romans 12:19, NLT)
`Page 87

River Street Savannah, Georgia
Over two hundred years ago, the warehouses lining the famous tourist district, Savannah's River Street, were filled with cotton and enslaved families. Some have said that you can still see the marks and remnants on the walls where slaves were chained as they waited to be sold and auctioned as property.
Page 18

S

Selfish Ambitions
It is my opinion that true shepherds of God are selfless leaders, whereas the bullying autocratic church leaders are selfish, only interested in themselves at the expense of others
Page 14

Shepherds African American churches
The African American churches
during the era of civil rights were led by some of the greatest
theologians and true shepherds of God,
Page 12-15

Sinful mountains
My neighbor, the no-respect lady, knew my wife was gone
and so was her husband, so she decided to try her sinful mountain climb with me.
Page 32

Spiritual warfare
Our valleys may be spiritual warfare or the actions of others or
because of our rebellious actions, hate, or even due to the hands
of God Himself for our disobedience
Page 65

Storms and rain
"Some storms and rain in your life are to wash away the things
in your life you don't need."
Page 76

Summertime, Song from Porgy and Bess
"Summertime, and the living is easy…," from a 1933 song,
"Summertime," composed by George Gershwin for the opera
Porgy and Bess
Page 20

Switchblade
The nickname of the elderly man changing the tires was
"Switchblade." I asked my grandfather why they called him
Switchblade and he said, "The reason why they called him
Switchblade was because he carried a long pearl-handled
switchblade knife
Pages 21-22

Sword
Sword back into its place, for all those who take up the sword shall perish by the sword." (Matthew 26:52–53)
Page 11

T

Tears: Valley of tears
"Even when their paths wind through the dark valley of tears, they dig deep to find a pleasant pool where others find only pain. He gives to them a brook of blessing filled with the rain of an outpouring." Psalm 84:6
Page 97

Temptation
"No temptation has seized you except what is common to man."
1 Corinthians 10:13
Page 105

Temptation is not a sin
"Temptation is not sinning; giving into temptation
Page 105

The more we receive God's spirit
"The more we receive God's spirit, the less we will be threatened by the forces of spiritual darkness."
Page 138

Three spiritual warfare enemies
"In our spiritual warfare, we are faced with three enemies: the world, our flesh, and the devil." Eph. 2:1–3
Page 136

Tongue
A person's tongue can tell a lot about that person, just like when you go to a doctor and the doctor asks you to open your mouth to examine your tongue, which tells him whether you have a temperature, digestive problems, or another health diagnosis
"Remember your tongue will tell people a lot about you when you open your mouth." James 3:1
Page 36

Trials on earth
"Here on earth, you will have many trials and sorrows." John 16:33
Page 63

"Trust Others: If and when we place our trust in God, it will only be then that
we trust others."
Page 88

W

Walking through the valley
"When walking through the valleys of life, walk with God, for He will lead you on to your destination in life."
"When you walk with a man, you will only be going for a walk, and the man will lead you to your demise
Page 45

Women if you treat him
"Women: If you treat him like a king, he will become your king.
Page 42

Worrying and fear
When you lie down at night, you will not be afraid, your sleep
will be sweet. (Proverbs 3:24)
Page 55

When walking through the valleys of life, walk with God, for
He will lead you on to your destination in life.
When you walk with man, you will only be going for a walk, and
man will lead you to your demise